1ØØ THINGS EVERY CATHOLIC TEEN SHOULD KNOW

BY MARK HART AND TODD LEMIEUX

LIFE TEEN

Authored by Mark Hart and Todd Lemieux

Designed by Casey Olson

Copy editing by Rachel Peñate and Joel Stepanek

A special thanks to all those who have contributed to this resource in its original form.

Copyright ©2015 Life Teen, Inc. All rights reserved. Published by Life Teen, Inc.
2222 S. Dobson Rd. Suite 601
Mesa, AZ 85202
LifeTeen.com

Printed in the United States of America. Printed on acid-free paper.

TABLE OF CONTENTS

INTRODUCTION

Every Sunday around the world, hundreds of millions of people gather together for Mass. We might be separated geographically, but we are united spiritually. We speak different languages, sing different songs, and dress in different clothes; but the core of what we celebrate, the readings we proclaim, the prayers that we offer and the Eucharistic meal that we take part in unite us as one, holy, Catholic, and apostolic Church.

We are a family. God is our Father. Jesus is our brother and Savior. The Holy Spirit is our protector and guide. Our Mother is Mary. Our ancestors are thousands of saints. Our shepherd is the Pope. Our Sacraments offer us personal encounters with Christ. Our Church is a light of truth in the darkness of the world.

As Catholics, we are one billion strong and growing. It's important that we understand, however, not only who we are as Catholics, but also what we believe and proclaim. Many people claim to be Catholic but don't live by what the Church teaches. Others claim to be Catholic but don't *know* what the Church teaches. For some, being Catholic is like being Italian or Irish or German: It's more a cultural designation than a system of belief and practice.

It doesn't matter how old you are right now. Whether you are a teenager or an adult, God is always ready to share His love and truth with you. Do you desire to know God and His love? Do you care enough to seek His truth about faith and life?

It's vital to say upfront that **this book does not have all the answers**. That is not why we put it together. It is not designed to answer every question you have; it's a starting point. It won't answer every single question in its entirety. Why? Again, it's a starting point. This book has many answers, but not all the answers. Take the time to look up the Scripture verses and Catechism references listed with each topic. Check out, borrow, or buy the various books listed as references. There are answers to all of your questions. You just have to be willing to do the work to find them.

The purpose in writing this book is to give very brief, quick responses to 100 topics that you hear a lot about or should know (at least the basics) about as you strive to live your Roman Catholic faith, daily. This is not a complete list. There are topics that are not here, not because they are less important, but because we had to start and end somewhere.

Don't look at this book as "all you need to know," but instead a bunch of stuff that is good for you to know. The better you know the history of your faith, the teachings of the Church, and the objective truth regarding matters that the world debates, the better equipped you will be to serve God and to love the people around you.

God desires for us to be disciples (students) first, and apostles second. Before He can "send you out" (as an apostle) to share His good news, you need to "sit at the Master's feet" (as a disciple) and hear what He has to tell you.

Keep this book with you. Carry it in your car or your backpack. Flip through it when you have a few minutes here and there. Refer back to it when friends and family members have questions. Use it in conjunction with your Bible and be sure to have a Catechism handy. Lastly, take some time to go online to www.lifeteen.com for more information on these topics and for more materials (in the store) to help you grow in and share your faith.

We at Life Teen are here to help you. We are praying for you daily. If you have specific prayer requests, whether you are a teen or an adult, visit our website and let us know. Know that you are always welcome to join us. Find a Life Teen program in your area by searching on our website. Check out our summer camps and conferences that we host around the country. Look for opportunities to join us at national and regional trainings, retreats, and rallies. Life Teen is a movement of the Holy Spirit, and He's taking us all over the world. Wherever the Spirit leads us, we will go. Wherever we go, you are welcome! Life Teen is here to serve you.

Realize that you are never alone. Jesus promised you that He would be with you always (Matthew 28:20). He is around you in other people. He is present to you in His Word. He is available in the Sacraments. He is accessible in prayer, any time of the day. And He is truly present in the Eucharist, in every Catholic church on the planet. Go to Him. Let Him love you.

May our Lord Jesus bless you, and may our Mother Mary swaddle you tightly this day,

Mark, Todd, and the rest of the Life Teen Staff

1. THE BLESSED VIRGIN MARY

It doesn't seem right to give Mary only one page in a book about things you need to know regarding Catholicism. Mary *is* Catholicism. She is the perfect disciple. She is everything we are called to be. While we'll never be perfect like Mary, our pursuit of Christ should lead us to saintliness like hers: rooted in humility, trust, service, and love.

Life Teen is consecrated to the Blessed Virgin Mary. She is our guardian and our Mother. We ask her daily to pray with us and for us, and we encourage you to ask Her to do the same for you.

A popular question from people, especially non-Catholics, is, "Why focus at all on Mary? Why not just focus on Jesus?"

Often, the question is asked with sincere intentions, but stems from an erroneous idea that Catholics take their attention off of Jesus to focus on Mary.

At no time has the Catholic Church ever suggested taking the attention or focus off of Christ. We as Catholics and Christians, are encouraged, implored, and commanded to look to Christ and focus on Him in our prayers.

The misunderstanding comes in when people think that Mary takes the place of Christ, which she does not. Nor does our invitation to Mary to pray for us get in the way of Christ's work on our behalf.

Mary doesn't get in the way of Christ being our mediator to God. She enhances it.

When we pray, we invite Mary to join her prayers to ours, praying with us to Christ. Mary does not **and would not** do anything to divert the glory away from Jesus. She lived to glorify God. Anyone who disagrees should read **Luke 1:46-56**.

A few things I share with or ask people who pose this question to me:

When Mary came to Christ with a need (John 2) did He respond to her? Yes.
Did Jesus hold Mary in high esteem, honoring her like a Son should? Yes.
Did Jesus give her to us as a mother (John 19)? Yes.
Did Mary hold a place of honor in the early Church (Acts 1-2)? Yes.

God the Father calls us to be like Christ – to follow Him, emulate Him, love and serve and forgive like Him. It tells us in Scripture (Galatians 2:20) that we become "little Christs" when we follow Him. We are called to imitate Christ in every way (1 Corinthians 11:1). I want to be just like Jesus.

In prayer, ask Christ to grant you His Heart...

Pray:

I want to have the heart for God that you have, Jesus
I want to have the heart for the poor that you have, Jesus
I want to have the heart for sinners that you have, Jesus
I want to have the heart for the Word that you have, Jesus
I want to have the heart of mercy that you have, Jesus
*I want to have the heart **for Your Mother** that you have,*
Jesus

I have yet to find someone who truly prays that prayer who does not hold Mary in the beautiful esteem that she, as the Mother of God, deserves.

May Our Lady bless you and may her prayers be with you as you read and pray through this book. She will hold you and walk with you, whenever you call upon her, always directing your path perfectly and gently back to her Son... like a good mother does.

Our Lady of Life Teen, pray for us!

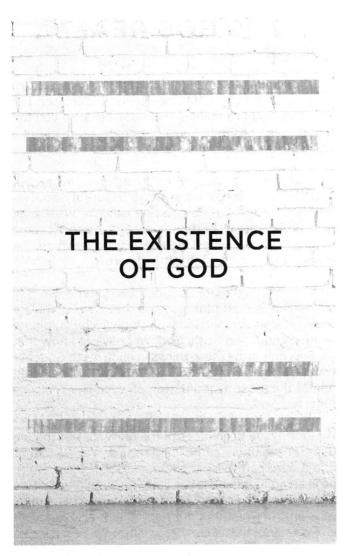

THE EXISTENCE
OF GOD

2. IS GOD REAL?

Man has always felt that tug towards the divine, toward something out there that he cannot understand but wants to. You are holding this book because you felt that tug — a desire to know something more about a world you might not know a lot about.

Our culture is always trying to achieve the bigger, better deal. We want the most beautiful spouses, the most money, the biggest houses. We want a lot of stuff! Despite all of this, man wants more. At some point, even the richest people on the earth realize there is more to life than getting more.

This something more is God. Every time we say something is beautiful, good, or even right, we are saying it is in comparison with that which is ultimate beauty, good, and truth: God. We may not know that we are comparing these things in our lives to God, but we are. This is why Mother Theresa was considered one of the most beautiful women ever. Her radiance reflected God.

We look at the beginnings of the universe – at the Big Bang, at evolution, at the fossil record – yet we cannot find the human spirit, the human soul. If you were to be in an accident and lose a limb, you would be no less the person you are today because you are not simply your limbs. When you are happy, sad, or overjoyed, it is your soul that feels these things. We feel it when we see the sun rise. We feel it when we look upon great works of art. We feel it when we hear music that moves us to tears. In some way, in some sense, these all reflect a small portion of the beauty of God. Our soul unites for one small moment with the divine.

Yet we can only know God if He tells us about Himself. We can no more understand God than an emu understands the human heart. So, we start on the journey to know God through what He has told us about Himself...

REFERENCES

Hebrews 11:6, Psalm 10, 19:2, Romans 1:19-20, John 14:9-11, 10:29-30, Genesis 12:7, 1 Kings 3:5, Isaiah 6:1-5, Ecclesiastes 3:11, Jeremiah 23:23, Ezekiel 43:1-5, Daniel 7:9

CCC 31, 33-5, 46, 48

3. GOD ISN'T PLAYING GAMES

There is always going to be something bigger and better when it comes to the video gaming industry. I came to that conclusion as another sleepless night left me red-eyed and yearning for coffee. Just when I thought I had achieved video game perfection, another level presented itself and I had to play on. Time passed: two in the morning, three in the morning, four in the morning. When the sun started to rise, I knew I was in trouble. No sooner had I beat that game when another hit the discount rack at the local store.

Does God ever lose sleep over me? Would God ever sacrifice His time in order to see me get to the next level of intimacy with Him? Am I just like a video game to God? I hope not. I play video games until I am done, and throw them away. God's love is more permanent than that.

The Xbox can never choose to not play. If I press the "Power" button, it is obligated by the rules of electricity and computer programming to function as designed. It would continue to function until it blows up or I turn it off. It has no choice in the matter.

God created me differently. God gave me a choice. I can play the game as offered by God, or play my own game. I can live by the rules He gave me or live by my own.

He has actually given human beings the ability to reject Him, and His love only requires one thing from us: a choice. We can either choose God, or choose ourselves. How ironic that the one who gave us the choice allows us to choose to reject or accept Him.

REFERENCES

John 3:16-17, 16:27, Romans 5:8, 1 John 4:8, Genesis 22:2, Joshua 22:5, Hosea 6:6, Ezekiel 16:8

CCC 313, 850, 2577, 735, 421, 321

4. FAITH AND DOUBT

There is a diary of a woman, considered one of the holiest in the modern era, which was released to the general public upon her death. It is riddled with statements of doubt about God.

"I feel that God does not want me, that God is not God and that He does not really exist.... My smile is a great cloak that hides a multitude of pains."

Surely, this couldn't be the writings of a saint?

In fact, these writings are from the diary of Blessed Mother Teresa of Calcutta.

St. Thomas suffered from doubt and so did the other apostles. But they also had faith, which is the active response to God's call.

There is a difference between voluntary and involuntary doubt. Voluntary doubt is the type of doubt you bring onto yourself for the sake of doubting. Essentially, you know that something is taught as true by God or the Church, yet you claim to doubt it as if that protected you in some higher court of law.

Involuntary doubt involves a doubt about God, about His will, or objections about God that you find difficult to understand. These are much different because you are actively trying in your heart to find the truth, yet don't feel you have fully found it yet.

The difference between the two types of doubt is that one involves a hard heart while the other involves a soft heart. The hard heart wants nothing to do with God's will, as it would require a change and sacrifice on its part. The soft heart is open to what God wants to make of it. So, when you doubt, ask yourself if your heart is hard or soft.

REFERENCES

Matthew 14:31, Mark 11:23, Romans 4:20, 1 Corinthians 15:14-17, James 1:6

CCC 114, 644, 1381, 2088-89

5. GOD'S NATURE

God is pure spirit. As a spirit He is immortal, without end, but also without beginning. Everything is always present to Him and He exists outside of time. Since He exists outside of time, He does not change. Since He does not change, there is nothing that is missing from Him.

He is all knowledge, which is the knowledge of everything on heaven and earth that was, is, and will be. We as human beings have enough trouble understanding ourselves, let alone the person next to us, at any given time. God is such pure knowledge that He knows more of us than we know, and more of others than they could ever reveal to us.

He is all love, which is the choice for the ultimate good for all, at all times. God's love is creative, which is shown in the creativity of the universe and all that is around us. There is variety from the smallest creature to the most complex person. In all times, God's love has always included the gift of free will for humanity. In this way, our choice for God is a reflection of His choice to love us. God freely chooses us when He does not have to or has no need to. His love is given totally, holding nothing of His Divine Nature back from us. His love, like His promises, will never fail, as God never changes.

Truthfully, this description, and every description of God is going to fall short. Every time a human being tries to describe God, we are going to fall short of truly capturing His nature. This is because we are His creations, using a language created by us! This would be the same as a computer program fully describing the nature of its programmer using only the language the program was able to develop! Our God is so great, so intense, so beyond us, that our every word of praise, description, and understanding will only be a hint of His true nature!

REFERENCES

Exodus 3:13-15, Wisdom 2:23, 13:1, Acts 14:15, Galatians 4:8

CCC 202, 253

6. FREE WILL

When God created us, He gave us free will. This freedom is the ability to act or not to act — to do something, or to not do something. Since God is the perfect good, free will reveals its true goal and purpose when we choose the good in a given situation.

God will never prevent someone from using his or her free will and, in the end, it is through choosing good that we are able to realize there is an even greater freedom. As if we are discovering new rooms in a house as we choose the right doors to open.

The opposite of freedom is slavery and the opposite of good is evil, so if we choose evil, we will find that we are falling into a slavery— possibly a slavery to addiction, cycles of hatred and abuse, and other sins.

Now, some have wondered, "since God already knows what I'm going to do, is it really free will?" Think of it this way, perhaps: you walk into your kitchen and open the refrigerator. Inside the refrigerator is cake and leftover, three-day old vegetable stew. You have the freedom to choose either to eat. Your Dad walks in and sees you staring into the fridge... and even thought *he knows* what you are going to pick, it does not impinge upon your freedom to choose either one. It's an imperfect analogy but you most likely get the point.

God will always honor our free will; so if we want to be with God, desire God, and chosen for God, then God will honor that decision. We will be sanctified and glorified. If we do not desire God and have chosen against God, then God will also honor that choice and allow us to move out of His presence.

St. John Paul II put it this way, "Freedom consists not in doing what we like, but in having the right to do what we ought." Since everyone has free will, we are responsible for our actions. There may be some situations where a person's responsibility can be diminished or cancelled, but everyone has a right to free will and is responsible for his or her own decisions.

REFERENCES

Sirach 15:14, 23:10; Jeremiah 21:8, Exodus 6:6, Leviticus 15:13, Ezra 1:4,6

CCC 1734, 1767-68,1809, 1834, 1853

7. MODERN LIES ABOUT CHRISTIANITY

There are many modern lies that exist about Christianity, but there are two untruths that you really need to watch out for as you begin to grow in your faith:

Lie #1 – Christianity is about being a good person.

Lie #2 – Conversion is a one time event.

Why are these two lies so dangerous? They breed contentment and spiritual laziness (sloth). Nowhere does Christ say that following Him is about being a good person or a nice person, or "if you just believe in something, that makes it true." Never once in the Gospels do we see Jesus utter, "Hey everybody, just forget about what I said… do it your way, just as long as everyone is self-focused and happy." In fact, He was so "un-nice" in His boldness that it got Him killed. People don't crucify "good, nice people."

In addition, many people wait for that "St. Paul" conversion story in their own lives where there is a vision and a voice, they see God and never want to sin again. St. Paul didn't say he never wanted to sin again. In fact, he spoke a lot about the fact that he did want to sin and the struggle he went through each day not to sin.

Conversions are wonderful in that they lead sinful people to become good people or at least better people. But the harsh truth is that Jesus isn't calling you to be a good person. Jesus Christ is calling you to be a *new* person, a new creation (Galatians 2:20), not just converted in mind but transformed in body and spirit. That means admitting that the life you currently lead might not be the life you're called to lead. It means acknowledging that there are areas of your life in which you won't let the Lord be the Lord... (but when) we embrace change for a *who* (God) and not for a *what* (religion) the sacrifice takes on assurance, joy and longevity. If your transformation is rooted in a relationship with God, it can brave the unexpected storms of life.[1]

The reality is that you're not as good as you think you are. The beauty is that you are not as bad as you think you are, either. Remember, the goal is not good in the eyes of the world. The goal is holy, in the eyes of God. His opinion is the only one that matters.

REFERENCES

Galatians 2:20, 6:15, 2 Corinthians 5:17, John 3:3, 6-7, 1 Peter 1:3, 23, 3:15-16

CCC 2769, 525-526,1698, 1708, 1715, 456-457, 461, 463, 504, 1880

SALVATION

8. WHAT HAPPENS WHEN YOU DIE?

Death is scary for a lot of people. Not as scary as public speaking, according to some studies, but still scary. Hamlet refers to it as the "undiscovered country." Since the human body is mortal, it is inevitable that it will die. Ever since the original sin of Adam and Eve, we humans must now take a more difficult path towards unity with God. This path goes through the doorway of death.

We spend our lives forming our conscience and setting our free will to choose God or to go against God. Christ taught that He will look at us, and if He recognizes himself in us, we will be welcomed to Him. At the moment of our death, our will is set permanently — there are no longer any changes to be made. We will have finished the act of creation started at our conception.

Of course if we are given a chance to see God in all of His glory, no will would go against Him, but then it wouldn't be *free* will, would it?

If we die with that desire for God, yet there are some things on our soul that prevent us from being fully unified with Him, however, we go through a period of purging during which time our soul is cleansed. You may have noticed that "purging" and "Purgatory" are similar word. Neat, huh? Almost like that happened on purpose.

If we are set against God, He will honor our free will and not force us to be unified with something we want nothing to do with for eternity. Unfortunately, this means we would also be separated from everything God had a part in and may not realize were from God.

So, your challenge, my challenge, our humanity's challenge is to die with a pure heart, so we are joined in a common union (kind of like the word "communion..." again, maybe that happened on purpose?) with God as our soul finds its home!

REFERENCES

Romans 8:38, Deuteronomy 30:19, Revelation 20:13, Philippians 3:20, 1 Peter 1:4, 1 Kings 13:31, Tobit 4:3

CCC 1005, 1007

9. WHY WAS MAN CREATED?

In the beginning, our original "parents," Adam and Eve, received a tremendous gift from God. That gift was our soul. The soul is a "ghost," or a shadow of God. With it, mankind received two things: Intellect and Will. Intellect allows us to know about God and the world around us, and to use our reason to know ourselves. Will allows us to make decisions and judgments between good and evil.

God created us with the ability to know Him. This means that, despite the fact that we are humans and God is an immortal spirit who lacks nothing, we are still created with a capacity to know more about Him. God also created us with the ability to love Him. This isn't the "rainbows and unicorns" type of feel-good love, either. That may be part of it, but it is more about using our will to choose God.

When we know God and love God, we are able to serve God in our own lives. Now if you have been to school, you know that there is a certain amount of knowledge that is presented in your classes during the school day. However, you also know that remembering it all and using every bit of information is impossible. You also know from going to school that not everyone chooses to do what the teacher wants. As such, we see that not everyone does what he or she was created to do. We were created to know God, love Him, and serve Him. Even though we were created for that purpose, we can choose against that purpose. This is due to free will.

Why would God create us in this way? Apparently, He believes that, even though not all people do what they were created for, the people who do are worth it.

REFERENCES

Genesis 2:3-4, Wisdom 2:6, Romans 1:20, 8:19, Ephesians 2:10

CCC 1700-1707

10. ARE YOU SAVED?

It probably began as a "normal day" for Jesus. Great crowds were pressing in on Him as usual. As Jesus was leaving, He ran into a "human roadblock" (Mark 10:17). The rich young man ran up to Christ and knelt before Him, blocking His path, posing a question. He asked Jesus, "What must I do to inherit eternal life?"

This question is asked frequently in the Gospels and remains popular today. Some Christian denominations believe they have it all figured out and claim with complete certainty that they are "saved" (they are certain they will enter Heaven). Other denominations know "what it takes" to be saved. So, what exactly do we as Catholics believe on the matter?

Salvation is a gift. It is a free gift from God. That is absolutely correct. It is also a gift that we can choose to leave unopened. Picture a huge present sitting beneath the Christmas tree, the biggest one, adorned in gorgeous wrapping paper with your name on it, sitting unopened because you'll have to sacrifice everything else you have to get it. The gift is free. The exchange is clear. It's your choice.

The rich young man had done everything he could do on his own. The passage tells us that he followed the commandments. What he was not willing to do was sell everything and follow Jesus completely. He wasn't willing to abandon his way of life, surrender himself to

God's will and trust that God would provide. The rich young man wanted assurance at that moment that Jesus was going to take care of him. He wasn't willing to walk every day with Him without that assurance. He wanted Heaven, he just didn't want to have to sacrifice what Christ was calling him to sacrifice to achieve salvation. Do you get it?

The question "are you saved?" is very common within certain denominations of Christianity. Usually the person asking it is really wondering if you have a personal relationship with Christ. You may have also heard popular questions regarding your faith, like have you *"asked Jesus to come into your heart"* or if you *"recognize and have accepted Christ as your personal Savior."* These are usually very sincere questions, asked by sincere people. Don't ever let the phrasing or even the zealous intensity of some Christians freak you out, questions like these are usually asked with good intentions.

As Father Romero put it, you can say, "Yes, I *have been saved* by Jesus' death and Resurrection" (Acts 4:12, Ephesians 1:7). Then follow up with, "I *am being saved* through the help of the Holy Spirit in the Sacraments, walking every day with Christ, my Savior" (Philippians 2:12). Then add, "and I *hope to be saved* when Christ, my Redeemer, comes again" (Matthew 25:31-46, Revelation 20:11-15).

Grace is an unearned gift, but it can be rejected through sin (John 15:5-6). The Bible warns us that our sins after Baptism could exclude us from heaven (1 Corinthians 9:27). Lastly, the Bible teaches us that heaven is a moral assurance, not a guarantee (Romans 11:22-23).

The rich young man was challenged with a difficult reality that day. An eternal life in Christ requires a daily "yes" to God's grace, not a one-time "get into heaven free" response.

Sincerely, more than anything, we need to pray for one another, Christians and non-Christians alike. God is merciful, but not weak. We should never seek to take earthly advantage of His Divine Mercy.

REFERENCES

Matthew 18:21-35, 19:25-26, Acts 2:17-21, Joel 3:1-5, 2 Samuel 22:3,47, 1 Chronicles 16:23, Esther 6, Hebrews 3:14, Romans 2:6-8, 6:3-5, 23, 11:22-23, Galatians 3:27, 5:19-21, 1 Corinthians 6:9-10, 10:12, 15:1-2, 1 John 5:16-17, Mark 13:13, 2 Peter 2:20-21

CCC 169, 588, 600-602, 620, 980, 1066, 2091, 2744, 2851

11. THE TRUTH ABOUT SIN

When you sin, you die.

When you read the line above was your response, "Whoa, that was harsh"? If so, you're not alone. People felt that way in Jesus' time too. The Scriptures are filled with examples of people looking for loopholes. The Scriptures are also filled with situations where Christ (and His apostles carrying on His teachings) reminds people of this truth: sin = death.

Without being too negative, let's take a look at what sin does to us. Sin does primarily two things: It destroys our capacity to love and hinders our ability to receive God's love. Sin is death, whether quick or slow. We'll take a look at these truths one at a time.

1. *Sin destroys your capacity to love properly.* When we sin it is not private. My sin doesn't just affect me; it affects everyone. We all belong to God. We are His children. We all make up the body of Christ.

    You might be thinking, what about a sin like viewing pornography or masturbation? That doesn't affect anyone else. It doesn't? Masturbation is a selfish act, a disordered act. It affects our love of others and of self. Pornography destroys the dignity of the human person. It distorts how we look at the body, the opposite sex and God's gift and purpose of sexuality. Often, it is in the seemingly "private" sins that our ability to love properly is most compromised.

2. Sin hinders and eventually destroys our capacity to receive God's love. There is no sin you can commit that God won't forgive. The only sin God can't forgive is the sin you don't ask forgiveness for. It would be a violation of your free will for God to forgive your sins without permission.

You may have heard about sin against the Holy Spirit being unforgivable. That simply means that when you do not ask forgiveness for your sins or refuse God's mercy, you sin against the Holy Spirit. If you say, "my sin is too big" or, "I am too bad for God to forgive me" you have bought into a lie from Satan. No sin is bigger than God. Throw yourself into His arms of mercy.

So, sin is death. It is spiritual death, emotional death, social death, psychological death and eventually, physical death if we are too prideful to run to God's mercy. Think about it: If there were no cost, no consequence for sin, why would Jesus have paid such a price on the cross for us?

REFERENCES

James 1:14-15, Romans 3:21-23, 6:22-23, Psalm 1, Numbers 9:13, 32:23, Ezekiel 44:10, 12

CCC 1420, 1472-3, 1459

12. MORTAL VS. VENIAL SIN(S)

Given the choice between God and ourselves, human beings will choose themselves at times. Any one of us would agree, however, that some sins are bigger, more important, and probably more deadly than other sins. Understand that all sin, no matter how small, will eventually lead us away from God over the course of time. It is important to talk about the difference between the two types of sins: Mortal Sin and Venial Sin.

Let's start with Venial Sin, which is not deadly to the soul but is still an offense against God. It is pointless for us to debate if any sin is an offense against God since we are not the ones who make the rules. Let's just say that all sins are an offense against God. In the case of a Venial Sin, you may not be aware that you are committing it because you do not know it is wrong. It may be a knee-jerk reaction, without using your free will or intellect. You might do something without thinking at all about the consequences. The danger in Venial Sin is that we may not take it seriously or confess it because it is "just" a Venial Sin. In the end, that Venial Sin can become serious, turning our hearts against God if we do not tear the sin out at the root.

Mortal Sin does something that Venial Sin does not, which is the source for the name "Mortal." It can, quite literally, kill our souls. Since our souls need grace to survive with God in Heaven, much like an astronaut needs a spacesuit in space, we need to guard ourselves against losing this grace. A Mortal Sin removes all Grace from the soul. It is a deliberate refusal of God's gift of grace to us. We reject God at our very core.

One commits a Mortal Sin when it is a serious sin — we know it is sin when we consent to the sin.

REFERENCES

1 John 5:16-17, Lamentations 3:39, Psalm19:13, 103:10; Ezekiel 18:20, 1 Corinthians 6:18

CCC 1854

13. HOW GOD'S MERCY WORKS

What if God ever ran out of energy? What if God ran out of grace? What if God grew tired of loving? Luckily, you won't have to worry about those questions, because God is perfection. If God ran out of anything, He wouldn't be perfect, would He?

God is absolutely without limit. There's no limit to His love, power, or mercy. You and I should take great confidence then that God can and does hear all of our prayers, because God is *that* perfect, He is *that* big. However big your sin, God's mercy is bigger. However large your tears, God's Kleenex are larger. Your sin, however grievous, is a bucket of sand in the ocean of God's mercy. Don't keep your sin from the mercy of God.

God is always willing to forgive you. Forgiveness is awaiting you. The Sacrament of Penance is the answer. God's grace can always restore you, putting you back in right relationship with the body of Christ. Reconciliation is a beautiful gift; it makes you a living saint. Throughout the Bible we see God's children, children that He has blessed and whom He loves, turn away from God out of selfishness. We never see God run out of mercy.

Jesus did not die for your holiness, He died for your sinfulness (Luke 5:31).

Jesus Christ is waiting for you. He is not afraid of your mess. He is bigger than your sin. Confession focuses on the sin, Reconciliation focuses on the sinner. The Commandments are not the antidote to suffering, they are like X-rays, enlightening those areas within that need to change. Christ is the surgeon waiting to reconstruct those broken areas of your life, those areas you attempt to ignore or hide. Jesus is calling you — pick up the phone. Better yet, schedule an appointment and swing by His office.

REFERENCES

Luke 1:50, 1 Peter 1:3, 2:10, Romans 11:30-36, Jeremiah 16:13, Daniel 3:90

CCC 210-11, 270

14. THE SEVEN DEADLY SINS

The Seven Deadly, or "Capital," Sins follow the tradition of St. John Cassian and St. Gregory the Great. They are called "deadly" and "capital" because they are the root and source of all other sins and bad habits. So, let's take a quick look at the seven, what they are and all they encompass:

Pride: The original sin of Satan and Man and the sin that separates us from God the most. It is the idea that we know better, can do better, and would be better off if we were God. This is the most glorified of the sins today.

Greed: St. Paul calls this the "root of all evil." It is the idea that material goods can bring us happiness or heaven here on earth. Any time we put material goods before the will of God, we are creating a false god.

Envy: We are envious when we become upset because someone else has good happen to him or her. When we allow envy to set in, we become resentful because we think that we are just as good as anyone else and we deserve the happiness that others have.

Anger: We can all point to Jesus overturning tables in the Temple as an example of anger, but what we need to remember is that there is a difference between "anger" and "righteous anger." Anger is more then what is needed for the evil being fought. One only needs to look at the news to see examples of people letting their anger control them.

Lust: Entertaining the desire to use another person simply for sexual satisfaction is called "lust." It reduces another person to an object or thing when we should be bringing him or her closer to God. This is the most talked-about sin of the seven.

Gluttony: The desire to indulge in any type of food or drink to satisfy our hunger — even our hunger for heaven. We eat and drink as much as we can, letting our desire for food and drink consume us.

Sloth: The most misunderstood of the seven sins and the most "hidden." While laziness is often used to describe it, it is, in fact, an apathy toward God. When we are confronted with the Lord, who is the Creator of the entire Universe, we need to make a decision about what we are going to do. Those who commit the sin of Sloth decide to sit on the fence, not committing either way.

The only antidote to sin is grace and if you're looking for grace, you've come to the right Church... the sacraments (all SEVEN of them) offer grace – which is God's very life – more directly and fully than anything else in creation.

REFERENCES

Proverbs 6:16-19, Exodus 10:17, 1 John 5:17, 1 Corinthians 6:18, Ezekiel 18:20, Ecclesiastes 7:20, Jeremiah 5:25

CCC 2088-89

15. HEAVEN: OUR HOME

Heaven is eternal joy — our natural selves as they were intended by God. If we die, our wills are turned toward God and we have the grace of God in our souls, then we are unified with Him for all eternity. Our heart's deepest longing is satisfied in God. We are joined with the saints and angels and see God "face to face," according to St. Paul (1 Corinthians 13:12).

We do not become angels in heaven because we are not angels. We are human beings. God, as the perfect good, the perfect knowledge, and the perfect love, gives us our fill of each. Since each human being has a different capacity for each of these (good, knowledge, love) during the course of their lives, we all experience them in different amounts in Heaven. I won't know the difference between the Heaven I experience and the Heaven you do, as we will both be perfectly satisfied.

Read and re-read **1 Corinthians 2:9**. Pray it. Commit it to memory.

God wants everyone to be in Heaven. He wants it so much that He died on the cross in order that we may be with Him. The only thing keeping us from Heaven would be us. We can change that any time we want by giving ourselves completely to the Lord of Heaven and Earth.

REFERENCES

Isaiah 6:1-8, Genesis 6:2-4, 1 Kings 8:22-23, Psalm 2:4, 11:4, 14:2, Isaiah 24:4, Revelation 21:10

CCC 32, 1821, 2053, 2796

16. PURGATORY: A REALITY

Many non-Catholics have questions about purgatory because they feel it has no basis in Scripture. However, there are several Scripture passages that support the doctrine of purgatory.

It is correct that the word "purgatory" is never mentioned in Scripture. At the same time, the term "Trinity" is not mentioned in Scripture, either. In fact, if you want to get technical, "Bible" isn't even Biblical. It only appears on the cover and cover pages, and not in the actual text.

The verb *purge* (from which we derive the term purgatory) comes from a Latin term meaning "to purify." Literally, purgatory is a state of cleansing where our souls are purified from sin through intense measures.

Revelation 21:27 clearly teaches that "nothing unclean will enter Heaven." Likewise, in 1 Corinthians 3:15, St. Paul states that "if someone's work is burned up, that one will suffer loss; the person will be saved, but only as through fire." The burning below cannot refer to Hell, because in Hell people are not saved.

Jesus Himself teaches us that some sins can be forgiven in the "next world," as we hear in Matthew 12:32. This "middle state" is described elsewhere in Scripture too (1 Peter 3:18-20, 1 Peter 4:6). St. Paul prayed for the dead too. Just read 2 Timothy 1:16-18.

In addition, there is a passage in 2 Maccabees 12:44-46 which clearly speaks of the existence of purgatory. You'll notice that 2 Maccabees is a book not included in non-Catholic Bibles, but we'll discuss that more in a later question.

The question shouldn't be, "Where in the Bible does it discuss purgatory?" but rather, "Why the need for purgatory?"

God is perfect holiness (Isaiah 6:3). We are called to be perfectly holy (Matthew 5:48, 1 Peter 1:15-16). Without perfect holiness, we cannot see God in Heaven (Hebrews 12:14). Purgatory is not meant for our pain, but for our cleansing and sanctification (Hebrews 12:11). All discipline and affliction leads us closer to God, if we let it (Romans 5:3-5, James 1:2).

Yes, Christ did accomplish all of our salvation by dying on the Cross, but the Scriptures teach and remind us that it is through *sanctification* that we are made holy over time, and through other ways that can involve and include suffering. Purgatory is just the final stage of sanctification for any of us in need of purification prior to entering the perfect and eternal banquet of Heaven.

REFERENCES

Revelation 21:27, Matthew 12:32, 2 Timothy 1:16-18, 2 Samuel 12:13-14, 2 Maccabees 12:44-46, 1 Corinthians 3:15

CCC 1030-32, 1472

17. WHY THE *HELL*?

As much as Heaven is the fulfillment of all goodness, knowledge, and love, Hell is the opposite. When we die, our wills are set. We have freely chosen in this life whether we want to be with God for all eternity. God, in His love, will not refuse our request.

We may think during this life that we don't need God — that we have the ability to be happy on our own, know things on our own, or be good to others on our own. When confronted by God, those who are destined for Hell cannot accept that all of those abilities come from God. They cannot live in a Heaven, where they do not "run the show." As they sink into their hatred and anger, they continue to blame God for the state they find themselves in.

Since they are in a place removed from God, there is no way for them to know His will or anything about His plan. They are eternally frustrated by their own ignorance of God and each other. There is no goodness either, with people simply using those around them in order to seek some type of pleasure they can never find. This hatred and ignorance is compounded by the lack of any love. There is no sacrifice, no beauty, no joy. There is only selfishness, ignorance, and hatred.

REFERENCES

Matthew 22:12-14, 25:41-46, Luke 3:9, 16-17, John 15:6
Isaiah 33:11, Job 1:6-9, 2 Kings 1:2-6, 1:16

CCC 1033-36, 1861

18. WHY DID JESUS HAVE TO DIE ON A CROSS?

God loves you so much that He would rather die than risk spending eternity without you.

Do you believe in the statement above? Read it again, pray about it, and ask yourself, "Do I really believe this?"

This is the reality of the cross and the reality of God's unyielding love. God loves you, not just the world, but you, intimately and personally. He loves sinful little you so much that He would rather take your sin upon Himself than write you off or risk losing you forever to a place where He is not (hell).

If you don't agree with this statement it means that you don't believe Jesus was God, that you are a sinner or that the cross of Christ and the mercy of God are bigger than your sin.

Whether we think we have sinned has no bearing on the fact that we have actually sinned. How "bad" we think our sin is has no bearing on the fact that sin is death (Romans 6:23). How merciful God is has no bearing on the fact that God is also just. *Don't mistake God's mercy for weakness*.

God is too just to dismiss our sin. God upheld "His end" of the covenant. He loves us perfectly. It is us, you and me, that fall and fail. Because God is just, He cannot simply dismiss sin. It requires an offering, a blood offering. If God simply forgot about our sin then how could we trust God or any of His promises (there are more than 4,000 promises God makes in the Bible).

Imagine the ramifications of that for a minute.

If God doesn't uphold the covenant broken in the Garden by Adam and Eve (and broken over and over again by His children since) then God is a liar or a pushover and we can't take Him at His word. That means not only is there no forgiveness, but no Heaven, no eternal life. That means that Jesus isn't God. He didn't rise from the dead. It means when you die, you die.

But as God promised us in the Garden, after the afternoon fruit snack where all hell broke loose (literally), He would send us a redeemer (Genesis 3:15). Christ is that redeemer. Christ is your redeemer. And that leads us to "the greatest checkmate in the history of creation." Here's why...

While God is too just to dismiss your sin, God is too loving to dismiss you. As a result, God came up with a plan, the greatest plan in history, to ensure that you have a shot at eternal life, a plan that both covers the sin (with blood) and opens the door to salvation.

Your redemption is more than simple forgiveness; it is adoption. It is God, your father (Mark 14:6) saying, "I've seen your sin and I'll take your place. I've seen your sin and I love you anyway."

God loves you so much that He would rather die than risk spending eternity without you. Can't comprehend this kind of love? Feel like your sin is just "too big?" Think again.

REFERENCES

Matthew 27:40-42, Luke 23:26, John 19:17-25, 1 Corinthians 1:18, 1 John 2:2, 4:10, Romans 3:25, Hebrews 2:17

CCC 606-618, 636-637, 571-572

THE MAGISTERIUM

19. WHAT IS TRADITION?

Tradition in the Catholic Church is the passing of truth to those who are learning about the faith, which we all are. Tradition can be taught by the spoken word or can be written down.

In the first years of Christianity and the Catholic Church, the people who referred to themselves as Christian had no New Testament. It had not been written, so early Christians lived by the word of mouth that was passed from one small community to the other. We hear about the apostles preaching to different churches in different areas of the world. St. Paul actually tells the Thessalonians to remember what they were taught by word of mouth and by the letters written to them (2 Thessalonians 2:15). Jesus himself never asked the apostles to write anything, but to simply preach that Jesus had risen from the dead and baptize all nations in the name of the Trinity.

Later, as the Scriptures came to be accepted by the Church, tradition assumed its full written form. What started with the tradition of the Old Testament was completed in the New Testament! That Tradition continued to be opened and expanded by those who had been given the authority to do so: the apostles and their chosen successors, the bishops. When the bishops are united with the Pope in matters of faith and morals, they speak with the authority of God, according to Christ's promise.

REFERENCES

Matthew 15:2-6, 2 Thessalonians 2:15, 3:6, 1 Corinthians 11:2, 1 Timothy 3:15, Sirach 8:9

CCC 75-79, 81, 84, 97, 174, 126, 1124

20. WHO HAS THE AUTHORITY?

Authority has seemed to be a very negative word since the 1960s, representing oppression of individual freedom and removal of rights. Unfortunately, we have missed out on the freedom that Authority offers.

Imagine you are playing a game of football. Everyone knows the rules, and on the last play of the game, your team throws a touchdown. However, the defensive team claims there was a penalty. From their point of view they are right, while from your point of view, you have won the game. Who is right?

If you answered, "the referee," you are right. The referee has the full authority in this case. They make a decision and everyone must live with it. You would be pretty angry if you thought the referee is wrong.

But what if the referee could never be wrong? What if the referee could always interpret every play correctly, no matter what?

You could feel angry at the outcome, but you would never say that it is wrong. You would have to submit to the decision and come to accept it.

The Authority in the Catholic Church is the same. Jesus Christ gave His authority to the Church to correctly interpret all matters in faith and morals. We have one of two choices in this circumstance. We can accept that the Authority of the Church comes from Jesus Christ and that it is much bigger than we are, giving us a freedom to play the game. Or, we can fight the referee and never get to play at all.

REFERENCES

Genesis 39:9, 41:35, Matthew 21:23-24, Exodus 23:21, Micah 3:8, Daniel 6:4, Hosea 8:4

CCC 88, 2036

21. WHY DO WE HAVE A POPE?

Why do we have a President? All right, bad comparison, given that there is no "Legislative Branch" (per se) in the Church.

Every company needs a CEO, someone to give it a guiding vision and pass that vision on to the people in the company. A good CEO points out where a company needs to improve in order to fulfill the mission given to it by the founder.

Jesus had 72 people who considered themselves His followers. Out of those 72, He had 12 who He worked with intimately to train them on how to preach, teach, and heal. Of those 12, there were three that He selected to be in his inner circle of friends.

Each of the three was given a special role in the Church. Peter was the "rock" on which Jesus would build His Church. As every group needs a leader, someone to cast the deciding vote, so did the apostles and the bishops. Simon Peter, the fisherman, rose to the occasion. In his line are popes who become saints and popes who were less than saintly. Yet, each pope has upheld the teachings of Christ.

Since Peter, we have been blessed with an unbroken apostolic succession; that is, we have had a successor to the chair of Peter ever since his crucifixion in the mid first century. Some claim that the Church, at times, had "multiple popes." That is not true. There has only been one *true pope* at a time. Certain times, however, found more than one person "claiming" to be the Pontiff. Anyone who says otherwise, needs to check their sources and their history.

REFERENCES

Matthew 16:18-19, Acts 15:7, Luke 22:32-34, John 10:16, 20:22, 1 Maccabees 16:24, Titus 1:5, 1 Timothy 3:1, 8

CCC 891-92, 100, 882

There is far too much about the Holy Father(s) to do the Papacy justice here, but if you'd like to learn more on the Scriptural roots of the Papacy, check out www.lifeteen.com.

22. WHAT IS THE ROLE OF VOWED "RELIGIOUS BROTHERS AND SISTERS"?

One of the greatest stereotypes in Catholicism is that of the "tough nun" who ruled Catholic school classrooms with an iron fist. If you ask Catholics from the generation or two preceding yours, they will tell you stories of the "pain and suffering" that they endured. Stories like these are often like stories about "wisdom teeth" (everyone has their story to share, it's usually more painful than anyone else's and a majority of the time, it gets exaggerated.) That isn't to say that some nuns weren't tough or that all stories are fiction, only that time has a way of making memories more "vivid." Take these stories with a grain of salt. Why?

Religious sisters and brothers deserve great respect. Sisters and brothers fascinate people. In a world ruled by selfishness and materialism, they are a bit of a mystery. How can they sacrifice so much for other people? How can they "give up families," or "wear those outfits," or "do such humble, thankless tasks for so many people, for so many years"?

Our Church would not be as large or as strong as it is today without so many religious who devoted their lives in such a special way to the teachings of Jesus

Christ. It's really more beautiful than mysterious, so let's take a slightly deeper look.

There are two types of vocations that God calls us to: the vocation of marriage or the vocation of celibacy.

There are some people that are called to serve the Church through the vocation of celibacy in a way that concentrates on service and care for the less fortunate. For example, some of those less fortunate can be children who need an education or adults who are sick and alone. Some celibates work as educators, dedicating their life to the teaching youth the Catholic faith. Others minister to the less fortunate who can't afford the medical care they need.

There are those who are less fortunate in a spiritual sense. They are poor and need to hear the Good News. Some celibates are missionaries, helping individuals to learn to care for themselves and recognize that they are cared for by a God who loves them deeply.

In this sense, these celibates are brothers and sisters in the Body of Christ. They have taken on the role of a "sister" or "brother" of Christ in a formal sense by dedicating their lives to service of the Church. They are the ones Christ speaks of when He speaks of the family members who hear His Word and keep it.

The next time you see a sister or a brother, thank them for their loving service and humble example. Take some time to pray about your own vocation. Seek out religious to talk to and ask them questions. God might be calling you. Your responsibility is to remain open to the call. If He wants you, do not fear. If He calls you, say, "yes" and you'll understand what Jesus was talking about (John 10:10).

REFERENCES

Ezekiel 38:16, 44:19, Ezekiel 46:20, Romans 12:1-2, Hebrews 12:1-2, Matthew 19:12

CCC 915-944

23. WHY DO PRIESTS AND RELIGIOUS DRESS LIKE THEY DO?

A priest really stands out in his collar, doesn't he? He's not out of place at Mass or around the parish. But in a restaurant, an airport, or at the movies and a priest walks in, he stands out. Not in a bad way, but everything changes, right? People become more aware of their language and their behavior. It's like "holiness" walked in and turned on the light. People start to scurry around to be sure that they are presentable now that the lights are on. Nuns in habits are the same way. When they walk into a room, the whole environment changes.

Why is that? Is there power in the collar or the habit? In a way, yes, but it's more than that. It's not like the color or the material of the habit transform people, but they do make a statement about the person wearing them. It's a statement that speaks of service and sacrifice. It doesn't claim that the person beneath is perfect, but that they spend their lives seeking the One who is perfect. It shows that they are willing to sacrifice for others and put themselves second; that is the definition of a hero.

The black cassock or clerics symbolize a death to self and a life in Christ. Priests put their own desires second for the good of the Kingdom. The collar is a symbol of humility, obedience, and slavery. The words "obedience" and "slavery" have negative connotations, but in the hands of the Creator and when put into the service of the Church, they quickly become admirable, heroic, and bold.

In a similar way, religious sisters wear a habit as a designation of their specific religious order and way of life, as well as their humility, simplicity, and unity. How beautiful is their example? Think about what a statement that dress makes about their vocation. It's kind of cool if you think about it, they don't spend thousands of dollars on a wedding dress they'll wear once. Nuns get to wear their wedding dress every day.

Other symbols like cinctures (rope belts), veils, and rosaries are powerful images that hold special meaning and designation for different orders. Bishops wear a mitre (that big cool hat) on their heads and carry a crosier (the walking stick that looks like a shepherd's staff) as symbols of their office and role as leader and shepherd.

Everything has meaning and purpose. The next time you see a priest or religious, stop them and ask them about why they wear what they wear and do what they do. You'll probably learn, very quickly, that although they dress a little differently now (for good reasons) that they once looked and dressed just like you.

REFERENCES

1 Peter 5:5, Acts 12:8, Jeremiah 4:30, Isaiah 22:21, Zechariah 3:4, Micah 7:14

CCC 916-944, 1549, 1567

24. WHY CAN'T WOMEN BE ORDAINED AS PRIESTS?

There have been some amazing advancements in the human race in the last hundred years. One of the most beneficial advances has been in the rights of women. Once women were not allowed to vote, own property, or even voice an opinion in public, we now live in a world where (in most places) women are free to follow the call that God has placed on their hearts without fear.

Unfortunately in our pursuit to make an equal world for everyone, we forget that the sexes are distinctly different. They are absolutely equal, but equal does not mean the same. There are still things that men can do that women can't do. There are still things that women can do that men can't do (and after witnessing childbirth firsthand, men should be thankful for that fact). This isn't an indication that there is something wrong with either sex, far from it. Differences are a great thing, there are just roles that are specific to men and specific to women.

One of the roles specific to men is the priesthood. The Church could no more ordain women then it could change the sun into the moon. The Church knows that there are women who can be pastoral by caring for and ministering to others. It isn't that the Church believes that women have nothing to add to the Church. It is simply that the priesthood is role for men because Jesus Christ came to the earth as a man.

Jesus could have come as a woman, but He didn't. He could have come as anything He wanted to, but He came as a man. So when a priest acts "in the person of Christ" in the Sacraments, he is literally allowing Christ to use his body to do His work upon the earth. Since Christ was a man and the apostles were men, all priests are men.

Keep in mind that the role of the priest is to serve. To be a priest for any other reason than to serve is contrary to what Christ intended when He instituted the office of the priesthood. If our desire is to serve Christ and the Church, God will bless that. We will find that we are happiest serving in a way that celebrates who we are, not who we wish we were.

Keep in mind that priesthood is not the highest calling: Sainthood is the highest calling. Not everyone is called to be a priest the same way not everyone is called to be a religious sister or called to be married. However, everyone is called to live as a saint.

Strive for sainthood, regardless of your gender or specific vocation. Sainthood is the goal and God's greatest hope for you.

REFERENCES

Ezra 10:18, 1 Corinthians 7:32-35, 12:4-6, Ezekiel 44:22, Matthew 19:12, Hebrews 3:1, 4:14, 6:20

CCC 1577-80

THE CHURCH: THE LIVING TRADITION

25. PENTECOST: THE BIRTHDAY OF THE CHURCH

While the "conception" of the Church occurred during Jesus' public ministry, the birthday of the Church came on the Feast of Pentecost in 33 A.D. Pentecost comes from the Greek (via Latin) for "fiftieth" day. We celebrate the Feast of Pentecost fifty days after the Passover. It takes place on the seventh Sunday after Easter.

There were many annual festivals commanded by God (Leviticus 23) that the Jews took part in to honor and celebrate God's blessings. Jesus honored them too. The feasts included Passover, the Feast of Unleavened Bread, the Feast of Tabernacles, and Pentecost, to name a few.

Prior to Christ's death and Resurrection, Pentecost celebrated the end of the harvest season. Farming was a main industry and festivals marked the key moments within the farming season. There were festivals that marked both the beginning and completion (Pentecost) of the season.

It was during the Pentecost festival following Jesus' Resurrection and Ascension that the Scriptures assure us something very special occurred. You can read about it in Acts 2.

The Holy Spirit descended upon the disciples in the form of a strong, driving wind. Tongues of fire appeared above their heads as they spoke in tongues and were empowered to go spread the Gospel. We see that the life of the Church is centered around the ministry of Simon Peter, our first Pope, whose key leadership decisions to guide the Church were made through the power of the Holy Spirit.

It's important to note that Jesus told us "it is better for you if I go" because God was going to send "the Advocate" (Holy Spirit). Can you imagine that? What can be better than having Jesus in the flesh with us? What about having Jesus in the flesh, by the power of the Holy Spirit, everywhere (the Eucharist) and not limited to just one man's body, walking around Jerusalem? How about having Jesus in the flesh, within you by the power of the Holy Spirit, through the valid priesthood and in the Sacraments of our Church?

The Holy Spirit is not a dove. The Holy Spirit is not wind. The Holy Spirit is not fire. Those are manifestations of the Spirit. The Holy Spirit is a person, the third person of the Trinity. The Holy Spirit is not a "lesser" God. The Holy Spirit is not "the other God." The Holy Spirit is God. The Holy Spirit is not limited or confined by anything. The only person capable of confining the Holy Spirit's power is you.

The Holy Spirit is powerful and the Holy Spirit is within you. Put those two together and what do you get? The Holy Spirit is powerful *in you*. Believe it because it is true. Unleash the power of the Holy Spirit within you, like the apostles did following Pentecost, and watch how God's glory is revealed in and through your life.

REFERENCES

Acts 2:1, 1 Corinthians 16:8, John 16:7, Tobit 2:1, 2 Maccabees 12:32,

CCC 732, 767, 696, 731, 1287

26. CATHOLIC *IS* CHRISTIAN AND HERE'S WHY...

"Are you Catholic *or* Christian?"

Have you ever been asked that question?

When you tell well-intentioned (but apparently poorly educated) people that Catholics are Christians their responses can range from shock to joy to defensiveness.

A popular misconception is that Catholic is different from Christian. That's a mistake. Some denominations even teach that Catholics aren't Christian. A lie like that must make the saints stop singing heavenly praises and shake their heads in disbelief.

The term "Catholic" literally means "universal." In 107 A.D., Saint Ignatius of Antioch became the first person (on record) to use the term "Catholic" when speaking about the Church. It's important to note that just because this is the first instance of the term on record, Ignatius was merely sharing what all of those in the early Church, including the apostles, understood and believed, a truth for which they lived and died.

St. Ignatius (or Iggy of Anti for short) understood something that many modern people don't understand: True Christians are Catholic because from the time the Church began, the Christian church became universal. If you were a Christian, you were a Catholic. You weren't just part of your little local church in your local city. If you were a Christian, a little Christ, you belonged to the larger body of Christ, the mystical body of Christ, the universal body of Christ, the one, holy, Catholic, and apostolic body of Christ.

St. Iggy reminded everyone in his letter to the Smyrnaeans in 107. He proclaimed the catholicity of Christianity. He continued to speak and uphold this long-understood truth until being fed to the lions in Rome around 110.

The Universal Christian Church, founded by Jesus Christ is the Roman Catholic Church. Built upon apostolic tradition and the Rock of Peter, our Church is 2,000 years old. The Roman Catholic Church is the only Church begun by Christ, Himself. Every other Christian denomination is an ecclesial community, begun by a man or woman. That is historical fact.

REFERENCES

Matthew 16:18-19, 1 Corinthians 1:2, 14:12, Ephesians 1:22, 5:30-32, 1 Maccabees 3:37, 4:35, 6:63, John 17:17-23, Colossians 1:18, Romans 12:4-5

CCC 2837, 1292, 855, 1200-1208, 832-836

27. CATHOLICISM WAS ILLEGAL?

The year was 313 A.D. The Roman Empire stood alone as the greatest world power. At this time, Christianity was still illegal. Christians (Catholics that is, since all Christians were Catholic back then) were a persistent "problem." Even after hundreds of years of persecution, torture, and murder, the Romans were unable to completely extinguish the Christian Church. Great saints continued to rise up. Countless martyrs gave their lives, refusing to bow down before false gods or to worship anyone other than their true king, Jesus Christ. It was a difficult time for the Church.

The Roman Empire was so vast that it had more than one emperor. In 306, a man named Constantine was proclaimed an emperor. Constantine was no friend to Christians during his childhood or even when he was proclaimed emperor.

After years of prayer by his mother, Saint Helena, Constantine finally had a conversion experience. In a dream, the symbol for Christ appeared to him. He later had this symbol emblazoned on his soldiers' shields. The battle that followed was one of the greatest historical battles of late antiquity, the Battle of the Milvian Bridge (312 A.D.). The victory made Constantine the sole ruler of the western half of the Roman Empire.

In the spring of 313, Constantine met with Licinius (the eastern emperor) in Milan, Italy and together they developed a religious policy that legalized Christianity. That policy has come to be known as the Edict of Milan. Catholics were soon free to live their Christianity without fear of punishment or death. History tells us that Licinius later turned on the Christians, enacting laws that made it more difficult for bishops to serve and Christians to worship. Soon after, he turned on Constantine too, and was eventually captured and put to death. Constantine was baptized prior to his death and maintained Christian freedom for the remainder of his rule. Looking back, Constantine was one of the most powerful mama's boys in all of history.

Never underestimate the power of a praying mother.

REFERENCES

Acts 1:8, Matthew 16:18-19, Ezra 6:11, Psalm 81:5, Hebrews 11:23, Jeremiah 34:8

CCC 1907, 2107-09, 2211, 1705, 1741, 908

28. THE COUNCIL OF NICEA? WHY IS *THAT* IMPORTANT?

The Catholic Church has had hundreds of councils over the past 2,000 years. Many are quite notable, and many not so much. But the Council that took place in Nicea, Italy in 325 A.D. is notable for several reasons. It's where the Church formalized our Creed, the Nicene Creed to be exact, which we still recite each Sunday at Mass. Notice that we said "formalized," not "invented" or "dreamed up." The Creed, the core of our belief system, was known and held from the beginning. Over time it was further "unpacked" and became more formalized, but that should not be misunderstood. What we believe – what God has revealed to us – has been consistent since the beginning. However, the depths of God's truth are revealed over time.

You might be saying to yourself right now, "Why is it important for me to know that?"

Well, the Church calls councils in response to things going on in the world. Often they are called to clarify what the Church teaches, especially in the face of heresy. In the early fourth century, a man named Arius taught, "there was a time when Jesus was not." In other words, the Arian followers believed that Christ was not equal to God the Father, but that Christ was the highest creature of God.

The Council of Nicea set the record straight. Our Church Fathers silenced the smack talkin' and dropped the hammer on the heretical teachings of the Arian following. The Church formally declared and defined Christ's "homo-ousious," which means "one in being." In other words, that Christ is eternally begotten not made, "...one in being with the Father." It's a profession that you probably recognize from the Nicene Creed.

Christ is no transformer. Half God and half man. Jesus is one hundred percent human and one hundred percent divine. Wrap your heads around that math equation, boys and girls. How cool is the Nicene Creed? It's a pleasant image. It's a "nice scene."

REFERENCES

2 Thessalonians 2:15, 1 Corinthians 5:12, 1 Timothy 3:15, 2 Timothy 4:1-6

CCC 195-197, 14, 184, 187-188, 192

29. FAMILY FEUD: THE GREAT SCHISM

Tommy sat in his Sunday school class surrounded by his seven-year-old classmates. The teacher asked the class, "What commandment talks about your mommy and daddy?" Mary, sitting next to Tommy, raised her hand and offered, "Honor your father and mother."

"Very good, Mary" replied the teacher, who then asked, "Okay class, now can anyone tell me if there are any commandments that discuss brothers and sisters?"

Tommy raised his hand and replied, "Thou shalt not kill."

Maybe you can relate to this story. Some families get along with very little strife. Other families tend to have a great deal of conflict. Do you ever fight with your brothers and sisters? Arguments or disagreements don't necessarily mean that you don't love your siblings, only that you don't quite see eye to eye on matters.

Does your family photo accurately portray your family? Does the picture of smiling siblings show the reality of life at home, with brothers and sisters poking, pulling, and prodding each other on a daily basis? Every family has some conflicts and the family of faith in our Roman Catholic tradition is no different. For the first fifteen hundred years of Christianity there was indeed one Church: the Catholic (universal) Church, but it was not without some family disagreements.

In the eleventh century, 1054 to be exact, the family disagreed over some key elements of the Catholic faith. One in particular was Papal authority. After great debates and exhaustive conversations, the Catholic Church split in two. This "split" is known as the Great Schism. The word "schism" literally means "split" or "cleft."

The East then became known as the "Orthodox Church" and the West became known as the "Roman Catholic Church." St. John Paul II, Pope Benedict XVI, and Pope Francis have continued to make it known, that it was their fervent desire to reunite the eastern and western Churches (rites). Pope Francis has continued with that very same message. Our Holy Fathers want the universal Catholic family united! This would essentially reunite all of the brothers and sisters in the family around the dinner table once again. In fact, that hope of reconciliation extends beyond just the Eastern Orthodox and Western Catholic Church. It extends to all Christians.

REFERENCES

Ephesians 5:30, 1 Corinthians 12:13, Ephesians 4:4, Colossians 1:18, Romans 12:5, Matthew 16:18-19

CCC 817-819, 2089

30. THE TRUTH ABOUT THE CRUSADES

There is a common misunderstanding about the Crusades, brought on by bad history, bad movies, and a bias against anything Catholic. Many believe the Crusades is a story of a big, bad, western Catholic empire flexing its imperial muscle to kill the innocents of the Middle East. Unfortunately, this is an exaggeration of some bad examples.

The Crusades were, essentially, defensive conquests that were meant to secure the rights of all Christians to go to places like Jerusalem, Bethlehem, and Nazareth, to worship Christ in the land of His earthly life and retrace His steps. Even today, churches in the region now known as Syria, Iraq, Jordan, Israel, and Saudi Arabia can trace their roots to hundreds of years before the Crusades.

For years, various tribes who had swiftly adopted Islam had protected these churches, temples, and shrines, even as Islam grew throughout the region. Islam threatened to conquer the Byzantine Empire, which included the Byzantine Church, who, until a few years before, had been Roman Catholic. (There still was a close alliance and hope that the two could be unified.) A European union of armies was able to drive back the Muslim forces from the borders of Byzantine and retake Jerusalem. Unfortunately, the good intentions of the Crusade translated to the idea that individuals did things that have been a source of embarrassment for Catholics for the last 1,000 years.

During the 200 years of the Crusades, Jerusalem changed hands a number of times and both sides in the Crusades were guilty of terrible massacres and crimes. However, it is a mistake to label only Catholic Europe as the aggressor. There were many European women and children who were sold into slavery and killed when cities were taken over. Whole religious orders were founded for the sole purpose of offering themselves as human ransom in exchange for those who had been enslaved. There were also religious orders that were founded to defend the cities and rights of those living in the Middle East.

Under the Catholic rulers in what became known as the Outremer, peace existed between all faiths at one time or another. The ideals of defending those who cannot defend themselves, and of defending the right to worship God, are noble ideals. Those are the true ideals of the Crusades.

REFERENCES

Joshua 24:15, Matthew 26:52, John 14:27, Ephesians 2:14, Psalm 43:1, 72:4, Isaiah 1:17, 41:10, Zechariah 9:9

CCC 2089, 465, 817, 2422

31. THE PROTESTANT REFORMATION AND THE COUNCIL OF TRENT

For nearly 400 years, the Reformation was treated with contempt and scorn by Roman Catholics. Many are still angry about it. For others, it has taken a somewhat "softer tone." Some see the Reformation as helpful on certain levels but with many problems, the greatest being that it splintered the Catholic faith. God never intended to have over 30,000 denominations of Christianity. The Scriptures affirm that fact (Romans 12:5, Ephesians 4:4, Colossians 3:15). Charles V was quoted as saying, "It is preposterous that a single monk should be right in his opinion and that the whole of Christianity should be in error a thousand years or more."

Yet, that was what Martin Luther claimed. It is easy for historians to exaggerate the faults of a Church that had an uneducated clergy, especially after the decimation of the population of Europe known as the Black Plague. There were scandals, indulgences were sold, and the clergy was not only largely uneducated, but, in many cases, immoral. None of this changed the truth that the Church had been passed down from God for over more than 1,000 years.

Martin Luther pointed out the offenses of a Dominican priest named John Tetzel who taught (wrongly) that you could buy your way into Heaven by contributing to the Church. Tetzel was a great preacher and had a large audience wherever he went seeking funds. The Church disciplined Tetzel and clarified the practice of indulgences, and for years tried to make peace with Luther, but it was not to be.

The Reformation became violent and resulted in the Council of Trent, where the Catholic Church made vast reforms, strictly defining what a Catholic is, does, and prays. These changes helped clarify things in a confusing time, but the Church has never been the same and we pray every day for the unity of all Christians.

REFERENCES

Ephesians 4:4, 2 Thessalonians 2:15, Romans 12:5, Matthew 16:18, 1 Timothy 3:15, Colossians 3:15, 2 Timothy 4:1-6

CCC 813-822, 406, 400

32. FAITH VS. WORKS

"Do you want proof, you ignoramus, that faith without works is useless?" (James 2:20)

Our faith, which is an active response to the call of Christ, is needed for our salvation. Our response to Christ is our acceptance of His sacrifice on our behalf. What separates you from those who do not have faith? Are you a nicer person? Do you swear less? Do you serve the poor? All of these actions on their own are defined as "works." Now, certainly, there can be those that have no faith in God but can do good "works." They can be good people, decent citizens, sometimes better then many Christians.

But what we must ask ourselves is, "can I be better?" Just because someone who has no faith is "good," it doesn't mean he or she cannot be better. How much more charitable could someone be if they had faith, believing that everyone they came into contact with was another Christ? How much more hopeful could one be if they had faith in Christ's sacrifice that would lead them to Heaven?

Now that we see that works on their own are good, yet insufficient, how can we say that faith without works is not the same? Christ asked us to share our gifts. Christ asked us to take our light out from under the bushel basket so that we could be a light to the world (Matthew 5:15).

What good is a faith that we do not share? What good is a faith that we keep to ourselves? What good is a faith that bears no fruit?

Rather than being Faith vs. Works, perhaps we need to work on making it Faith and Works. Sounds like a marriage made in Heaven!

REFERENCES

James 2:14-17, Galatians 2:16, 5:6, Romans 3:27-28, Hebrews 6:1, John 14:15, Matthew 19:16-17

CCC 697, 901, 161, 183, 846, 166

33. VATICAN II IN SIMPLE TERMS

In 1960, Saint Pope John XXIII shocked the world by calling all the cardinals and bishops to Rome for the Second Vatican Council (called Vatican II). The beloved pope told the Church to "open the doors and windows" and allow the Holy Spirit to move. The time of our Church being "closed in on itself" had ended, and with the urgent, newfound openness to the Holy Spirit came changes in the Liturgy, the priesthood, and the role of the laity.

Vatican II caused a great uproar and confusion for many people in the generations that preceded your own. Change often has a way of being embraced by some, but rejected by many, especially when you're talking about making changes to anything as personal as faith practices or to long-standing traditions of the Church.

There were too many things discussed at Vatican II to really explain (in detail) here, but there are plenty of great resources to read more about it. Put very simply, the Second Vatican Council did a few major things, including:

- Making it admissible to celebrate Mass in the vernacular language of the country, not just in Latin.

- Opened up new doors for ecumenical dialogue between the Catholic Church and other religions and denominations.

- Invited greater participation from the laity in the service of the Church.

- Moved to rediscover the charismatic dimension of our Church.

- Solidified the Church's stance and teaching regarding Sacred Scripture and Tradition.

- Created greater opportunities for ecclesial and lay movements and communities to advance the Church's mission in new ways, ushering in the new Pentecost that Saint Pope John XXIII had hoped would occur.

From the Council, two dogmatic constitutions came forth, one on the Church and the other on Divine Revelation. There was also a host of other pastoral documents, declarations, and decrees. It is worth noting that Vatican II was a gift to us all, but was not seen like a gift by many. Leaders and scholars over the years have debated about exactly what the Council really did. Many people have spent time trying to explain what was meant by the phrase "open the windows." Some saw it as an invitation to "allow the modern world of the 20th century *into* the traditional

Church." Others saw it more as an opportunity to "let the Holy Spirit *out* to the rest of the world, sorely in need of His guidance."

Given our 2,000-year tradition, it takes time to fully realize the effects of any one council. Councils have to be seen in light of history and other councils. The effects of Vatican II will be felt for centuries to come and will necessitate patience, dialogue, and understanding as Catholics who may struggle with change try to embrace new ideas.

REFERENCES

Matthew 16:18-19, 28:19-20, 2 Thessalonians 2:15, Romans 12:1-2, Acts 15:7, John 14:16, 16:7

CCC 9, 192, 250, 884-891, 882

34. THE CATHOLIC CHURCH AND OTHER FAITHS

For a long time, there were and still are a lot of hurt feelings regarding the split caused by the Reformation. Some of the language that was used was misunderstood and used to scare those who did not share the Catholic faith. That was wrong, and there should be some clarification.

One phrase that seemed to be tossed around without abandon was "no salvation outside the Church." People interpreted this as meaning Heaven is closed off to those who are not Catholic.

Recent Church documents indicate a different interpretation. There may be those in the world who do not even share a belief in Jesus Christ. They may know some things about God and what He expects, but their understanding is like that of a person reading only every tenth page of a book. As we get closer to the teachings of the Catholic Church, more of the book comes into view. While we may think we have all the information possible in reading every tenth page, we are missing out on most of the book and will have a hard time getting the point. The more pages we read, the more we will be able to understand.

Someone who is not Christian may be joined to God forever in Heaven (or "saved" depending on how you want to put it), but it is the action of Christ, within the Catholic Church, that makes this possible, even if they do not know it. We pray that all Christians come to the full unity that Jesus desired for all Christians, recognizing that, outside of the revelation that is Jesus Christ as interpreted by the Catholic Church no one could be saved.

REFERENCES

Ephesians 4:4, Romans 2:5-8, 1 Peter 1:17, Philippians 2:12, 1 Corinthians 10:11-12, Hebrews 10:2-27

CCC 816-822, 1271, 1636, 1259, 1261, 1816, 776-780

35. WHO WROTE THE BIBLE AND WHEN WAS IT ASSEMBLED?

If you went to a book signing at your local bookstore, you would probably see a line of people waiting to get the author's autograph and a personal inscription. Imagine going to a bookstore and getting your Bible signed by its authors. What would the scene look like? The Bible consists of 73 books, penned by 40 to 50 writers over about 1,700 years. It would take an hour just to collect all of those signatures. The reality would be, that while the writers were responsible for putting pen to parchment, it is the Holy Spirit who inspired the words. God is the author of Scripture.

Some people have a difficult time with the idea that God is the ultimate author of the Bible. It's safer and more convenient to say that people were writing *about* God, rather than acknowledging the truth — the Bible is the Living Word *of* God (Hebrews 4:12). Scripture isn't people writing "their take" about God, but rather God breathing words through the pens of men. Did God utilize the different talents and gifts for writing, communication, and storytelling of each author? Absolutely. He used their gifts the same way He still uses peoples' gifts in ministry every day.

The Bible is without error. It is the fullness of God's revelation. That does not mean we understand all of it. Over the centuries, the Holy Spirit continues to illuminate us with new depths of truth, deeper avenues into the heart of God through His Word. God is constantly revealing Himself to us in deeper ways. When people say that Scripture is the "fullness of revelation," it means that no other books or writings since the Bible can or would be held in the same esteem. The Bible was inspired in a unique way, at a unique time in God's plan of salvation and in history. No other work in the present or in the future, no matter how brilliant, will be held in the same esteem as the Gospels... they are *that* divine, *that* perfect.

While the Old Testament was already written, there were hundreds of written works to be considered when compiling the New Testament canon. The word "canon" means "measuring rod." Canon is the term used to describe which Biblical books "measured up" and were included in what we now call the Holy Bible. Dozens of "gospels" made their way around when the New Testament was being compiled, each with their own unique spin on the life of Christ... some accurate, most absolutely inauthentic.

There are a few important things to note here:

First, the New Testament was almost entirely oral tradition (shared through speech, not writing) in the years immediately following Jesus' death. You'll notice that the Church didn't come out of the Gospels, *the Gospels came out of the Church.*

Second, the writers of the New Testament belonged to the only Church Christ founded (they were Catholic) and they believed in the True Presence of Christ in the Eucharist, including St. Paul (1 Corinthians 10:16-31) who wasn't even at the Last Supper but who was taught about the tradition of the Sacraments through oral tradition.

Lastly, it was the universal (Catholic) Christian Church who finally put the Scriptures together in the form you know today. It took years to formalize the full canon of Scripture. Travel was difficult back then, communication was slow, transcription was costly, Christianity was deadly and the Church was exploding in growth. It took many years of prayer, conversation, discernment, and debate by bishops, scholars, and leaders to prayerfully determine (through the guidance of the author, the Holy Spirit) which Biblical books were truly inspired. That process of prayer, guided by the Spirit, gave us the commonly held canon.

Any non-canonical or heretical books were disregarded, for the most part, over time. Finally, at the Councils of Rome (382 A.D.), Hippo (393 A.D.) and Carthage (397 A.D.) the list of inspired books was set. It's the same list you hold in your hands (when you hold a Catholic Bible, that is) today. The Council of Trent (1545-1563) finalized the canon for us, but the canon was commonly held for more than 1,000 years before that.

REFERENCES

Mark 13:31, 1 Corinthians 11:2, Acts 20:35, John 21:24-25, Luke 1:1-4, 1 Timothy 3:15, 2 Thessalonians 2:15, 3:6, 2 Timothy 2:2, Romans 10:17, 1 Peter 1:25

CCC 78-97, 120-138, 106-107

36. WHY DO PROTESTANT BIBLES HAVE FEWER BOOKS?

People will often accuse the Catholic Church of *adding* books to the Bible. That's not only untrue, but the person who says it is not someone you'd want to help you study for that history midterm.

It is true that the Catholic Bible has more books (73) than the Protestant Bible (66). Both have 27 Books in the New Testament; it's the Old Testament that there is a disagreement over. Now, there are two different canons of the Old Testament: the Palestinian Canon (the Protestant Old Testament) and the Alexandrian Canon (the Catholic Old Testament). Why the difference? What books are missing from the Protestant Bible?

The books in question are all from the Old Testament: Tobit, Judith, Wisdom, Ecclesiastes, Baruch, I and II, Maccabees, and parts of Esther and Daniel. Since the Bible we have today did not fall out of the sky neatly bound in leather, it is important to look at where it came from.

The Hebrew Bible (the Old Testament) was written in Hebrew (imagine that) but as the Greek language became the more dominant language a translation of the Hebrew Bible into Greek was created by 70 Jewish scholars between 250-125 B.C. (which is where we get the name "Septuagint." It is Latin for "70.").

By the time that Christ was born, Greek was the common language of the Mediterranean world and so the Septuagint was very popular. Jesus, along with all of the New Testament writers, would have been familiar with the Septuagint. In fact, the Septuagint was the Old Testament that the New Testament writers used as a reference when they wrote their individual books (any time they quoted the Old Testament it was the Septuagint that they were quoting from).

This canon of the Old Testament was accepted as *the* canon for 1,500 years, until the Protestant Reformation. In 1529, Martin Luther (a Catholic priest who became the leader of the Protestant Reformation) decided to use the Palestinian Canon (39 books) as his Old Testament canon.

People will often accuse the Catholic Church of *adding* books to the Bible, but as you can see, it was a group of Jewish rabbis who *removed* books from the Bible and Martin Luther who accepted this removal of books. In fact, Luther wanted to remove even more books from the Bible, the Book of James and Revelation, which is *un-biblical* to do (Deuteronomy 4:2, Revelation 22:18-19).

So, if your Bible contains the 46 books of the Septuagint as the Old Testament, then you are using the same Old Testament canon that Jesus, the apostles, the

New Testament writers, and the Catholic Church has used for the past 2,000 years.

To put it simply, when you're holding the Catholic Bible, you're holding the original, the Director's Cut, with all the footage and all the special features; the non-Catholic translations are like the films that are resized and edited to fit your screen or the network timeslot.

REFERENCES

Revelation 22:18-19, Mark 16:15, 2 Peter 3:15-16, 1 Corinthians 11:2, 2 Timothy 1:13, Deuteronomy 4:2

CCC 120, 138, 81, 106-107

37. THINGS TO CONSIDER ABOUT LANGUAGE AND TRANSLATIONS

When you read the Bible, it is easy to get carried away with passages where "God says this..." or "Jesus says that... " We must be careful in doing so, because we need to keep in mind that what we are reading is a translation.

I'm not talking about French to English either. Think about William Shakespeare. There aren't many people that can understand his writing, yet we still refer to it as English. Go back even further to the original *Beowulf*, and you find a version of English that is unreadable to the average person. That is why we rely on translators to give us the story in a language we can understand.

In the case of the Gospels, it is important to understand that Jesus spoke in Aramaic. He most likely understood and spoke Greek as well, but, in the day-to-day operations of His ministry, He spoke in Aramaic. The Gospels were written in Greek. What we read in our modern Bibles is an English translation for the modern reader — not the original Aramaic that Jesus spoke, or the original Greek that St. Paul wrote in. Of course, we do put a certain amount of faith in the translators.

That is why it is important to look at the Tradition of the Church and how certain passages have been interpreted for 2,000 years. While we can look at our Bibles and make assumptions about how it should be read, that is like a small child looking at Mars through a small telescope in the back yard, then calling NASA to tell them that the planet is red. The child could learn much more by both looking at the planet *and* reading what NASA has already discovered. In the end, the child would be much more knowledgeable.

REFERENCES

Genesis 10:5, 11:1,7 Esther 1:22, 3:12

CCC 109, 112-114, 119, 129, 1093, 1177

38. SCIENCE VS. FAITH: A CONTRADICTION?

Christianity is impossible because evolution has made it impossible to believe in the God who created the world in six days!

Too many times, have we heard the eulogy of religion as proclaimed by science? That seems odd, considering the number of questions that science cannot answer and will not answer. One of those questions is, "why?"

Why did God create human beings? Why do human beings search for something bigger than themselves? Where is the human consciousness? Where is the human soul? How do we know that these two things exist? Why do human beings love? Why do human beings sacrifice themselves, even their lives for others? Why do we think that certain things are always good and certain things are always bad?

When we eliminate the study of God from our lives and restrict ourselves to scientific explanations, we are not liberating ourselves, making ourselves freer and smarter. We are restricting ourselves and making ourselves more ignorant.

There is certainly a lot to be learned from the sciences. All of them. Since God created everything, we have nothing to fear from science. Science offers us an explanation of how God accomplished what He did, but we cannot forget that science cannot tell us everything in the same way that a sculpture cannot tell us everything about the sculptor.

Science cannot tell us what is beautiful. Science cannot tell us what is good. Science cannot tell us what is truth.

It looks like we need faith after all.

REFERENCES

Isaiah 55:8-9, 1 Corinthians 2:5, Matthew 8:26, Luke 17:5-6, Acts 3:16, Psalm 119:105, 139:23

CCC 121-130, 139-140, 39-43, 48-58, 70-71, 159

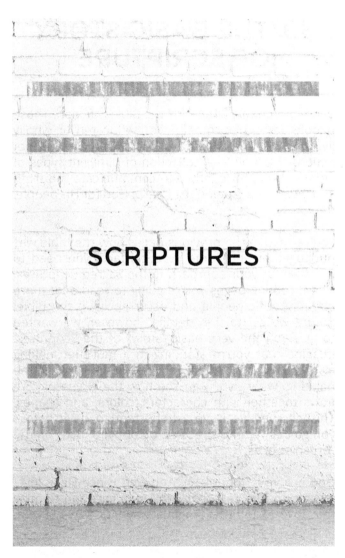

SCRIPTURES

39. THE BASIC STORY OF SCRIPTURE

There are people who think the Bible is fiction. Those people are either completely uneducated or wholly living in denial of historical facts. The Bible is not fiction. The Bible is a collection of different types of writing, brought together to communicate the truth and, more to the point, the love of God for His people, for you.

You've read in the previous pages how the Bible was put together and some practical facts you need to know about your approach to the Sacred Scriptures. In the coming pages you're going to read a lot more about specific people and occurrences in the Bible. Before we get to the "details," however, we wanted to give you the very basic "story" of the Scriptures. Imagine that you're standing in a museum looking at a painting. This topic is the "broad stroke" of the painting, where you can see how the whole picture flows together with characters, colors, and shapes. This perspective is very important to have before you go deeper into specifics, before you focus on the "brush strokes."

God is love (1 John 4:19). And God, since He is love, desired to manifest that Trinitarian love and to offer that love to us in a tangible way (*CCC* 293-295). St.

Bonaventure said that God created us "not to increase His glory, but to communicate it."

Love desires someone to love. God created the universe and all living things. And while all of creation is a reflection of the love of God, only man was gifted with free will. God formed a covenant with mankind (Adam and Eve) and gave us a sign of the covenant, the Sabbath. Man and woman chose self over God; they sinned and literally all hell broke loose. At that time, however, God also promised us a redeemer (Genesis 3:15).

Ever since "the fall," God has been working to get us back to Him. God's desire is to have all of His children gathered back to Him and with Him in our Heavenly home. Through a series of covenants, God continues to give us every opportunity to live in "right relationship" with Him. We are called to live in His love and to act in it; we are called to live as saints. Life is the pursuit of and desire for sainthood.

You're going to read of major characters like Noah, Abraham, David, and Mary. You'll read of minor characters like Rahab, Gideon, Hosea, and Philemon. Some are vital to know about, some are interesting to learn about, but all are important pieces to the greater puzzle.

The Bible is filled with characters, both saintly and "un-saintly," all embroiled in the same battle against sin as you and I are, every day. Don't make the mistake of thinking that "character" means fictional, however, as you too are a character in God's story of salvation (1 Peter 1:9). You are not an unnamed person in the story of creation. You are not an "extra." You are a primary character. God knows your name (Isaiah 49:16). God created you (Psalm 139:14-16, Jeremiah 1:4-8) and knows everything about you (Matthew 10:30, Isaiah 55:8-9).

You can find a little of yourself in every person in Scripture, man and woman.

You'll also read of epic battles, sin-filled failures, heroic lives, and miraculous encounters. These are real. They are true. They are not designed to "wow" you into loving God, but to remind you that He is God and that you are not.

The point is not to get lost in the details of the Scriptures, but to let the details give you even greater confidence as to their importance, insight, validity, and accuracy. Soren Kierkegaard once said, "The Bible speaks to me and the Bible speaks about me." With every turn of the page you'll find that one, the other or both are true.

Everyone loves a good story. There are plenty of books that don't move hearts or challenge minds. There are even more movies that are utterly forgettable, causing you to feel like you just wasted two hours of your life on the couch. The Word of God will challenge you. The Word of God will inspire you. The Word of God will give you hope. The Word of God will bring you joy. The

Word of God might confuse you, too. So, take some time and read through the next few pages.

And always remember to pray first, asking the Holy Spirit, the Author of Scripture, to open your mind and your heart to receive what God wants to tell you.

Stop by the Life Teen website, *www.lifeteen.com*, for more resources, hints, answers, and guides on how to start reading and understanding Scripture more. Check out the Life Teen store, too, for resources designed to help you better understand how to read the Bible, as you start to go deeper.

REFERENCES

Deuteronomy 4:6-9, Psalm 119:123, Genesis 3:15-19, Hebrews 4:12, 13:7, Mark 1:15, Luke 4:21, Joshua 1:13

CCC 81, 280, 1080, 431, 430, 668, 1103

40. WHAT IS A COVENANT (AND WHY DOES IT MATTER)?

A "contract" is an exchange of goods. I am in a contract with a car company. I give them the goods of money and, in turn, they give me the goods assembled as a car. I have nothing personally invested in the company besides the money I give them, and they have nothing personally invested in me and my life besides the car. Outside of the car and the money, we really have nothing to do with each other.

A "covenant," on the other hand, is an exchange of persons. Two people promise themselves to each other and give of themselves in a mutual act of sacrifice. The Scriptures are a story of the covenants that God made with man. The series of covenants, in a nutshell, follow:

God and Adam: God gave Himself to Adam in the Garden of Eden, which was reflected in the marriage between Adam and Eve.

God and Noah: God gave Himself to Noah on Mount Arrarat after the flood, promising to redeem mankind without destroying it. This was reflected in the rainbow.

God and Abraham: God gave Himself to Abraham in the wilderness and promised that Abraham would be the ancestor of a great nation of kings and of the Messiah. This covenant was sealed through circumcision.

God and Moses: God gave Himself to the nation of Israel through Moses in the desert, before they entered Canaan. God promised to bless the new nation with a land of their own and the Messiah. This covenant was shown through the law that was passed from God to the nation: The 10 Commandments.

God and David: God gave Himself to David and his kingdom, blessing his family and revealing that David will be the ancestor of the Messiah. This was represented in the building of the Temple by Solomon. God and Jesus: God gave Himself to all of humanity through the sacrifice of Christ. This marked the beginning of the Catholic Church as the eternal kingdom established by God.

The Final Covenant: At the end of time, there will be one final covenant when the natural world will pass away and our glorified bodies will be joined with our souls in union with God forever.

REFERENCES

Nehemiah 4:9, Judith 8:14, Psalm 83:13, Luke 7:30, Matthew 26:26-30

CCC 357, 73, 2176

41. GOD'S CHOSEN PEOPLE

After the fall of Adam and Eve, God set into motion a plan to save mankind from our sin. That plan involved a Messiah, a perfect sacrifice who would be willing to take on the sins of the entire world.

In order to bring the Messiah forth, it was important that there be a people for this Messiah to be born into, who would understand the sacrifice and give him a background, and to whom God would reveal Himself to in a special way.

From a time when mankind consisted of violent, wandering tribes and a few cities, God carved out a place for the Messiah. The result was the Israelites. Starting with Abraham, the nation was eventually torn from the land of Egypt, where they were slaves, and formed in the desert.

God guided them throughout their history and promised them that they were the people He set apart to bring forth the Messiah. He referred to them as His "Chosen People," His "Bride," His "Flock." Through the nation of Israel, all nations will be blessed.

God did not change. He does not hold the Jewish people any less in His heart now than He did 3,000 years ago.

REFERENCES

Genesis 32:39, 33:20, 34:7, Psalm 14:7, Sirach 30:36

CCC 781

42. KEY STORIES OF THE OLD TESTAMENT

The Old Testament is the history that led up to the coming of Jesus Christ. Here are a few key stories you should know, and why:

Creation — Adam and Eve: If you don't know what happened at the beginning, what happens at the end will make no sense whatsoever. *Genesis 1-3* is profound and could be studied for years on its own.

Noah's Ark: The story of the flood is a classic and reveals God's loving justice in *Genesis 6:5-9*.

Abraham and Isaac: God asked for an impossible sacrifice from Abraham, and this one man's faith leads to the birth of a nation.

The Burning Bush: The call of Moses is a moving story of God reaching out in love and guidance to one who is scared but faithful to God.

The Crossing of the Red Sea: This event was a big miracle of the Old Testament when God rescued the Jewish people from the Egyptians.

The Walls of Jericho: The battle that started the Israelites invasion of Canaan is idiotic military strategy, but a brilliant faith in God and the story behind some great songs.

Samson the Judge: Killing lions and Philistines, the strongest man *ever* revealed the might of God manifested through a human judge.

David and Goliath: Faith in God through a young boy brought a mighty warrior to his knees, and began the public life of the greatest king in Israel's history.

Elijah on Mt. Carmel: God battled with the priests of a pagan god. Guess who wins?

Esther and the King: God worked through the most unlikely of queens in order to prevent the total genocide of the Jewish people.

REFERENCES

Genesis 1:1-3, 6-10, 15-23, Books of Exodus, Numbers, David, 1 and 2 Kings

CCC 128-129, 140, 1286, 1094, 702, 2130

43. WHY DID JESUS COME *WHEN* HE DID?

If we could look at history through the lens of Jesus Christ, it would be easy to see why God chose the time that He did. Sure, He could have taken advantage of the Internet and social media today, but would history have developed in the same way?

The Jewish people had recently gone through a revolution against the Greeks that solidified their identity as a people of God. The Old Testament had been assembled, and the Jewish people in Palestine had become a part of the Roman Empire.

The Roman Empire had come to power under the Caesars and peace reigned. There were roads throughout the Empire that could take you from Spain to Egypt in a relatively short amount of time. For the first time, news and people could travel quickly to people of all nations — news such as, "A savior has come!"

If Christ had come earlier, He would have been caught up in the transition between the Greeks and the Romans. Perhaps the apostles would have been swept into the wars, and the Gospel would not have spread so easily.

If Christ had come later, Jerusalem would have been destroyed by the Romans (AD 70) and there would not have been a centralized Jewish people for the Messiah to be born into. God's timing was, in hindsight, completely perfect.

REFERENCES

Matthew 1:18, 1 Peter 1:3, Luke 2, Psalm 102:13

CCC 479, 485, 497, 723

44. HOW CAN WE BE SURE ABOUT CHRIST'S MIRACLES?

Jesus once said, "Unless you people see signs and wonders, you will not believe." (John 4:48)

Many times, modern day followers of Jesus fall into the same trap. Maybe you've prayed for God to "show you a miracle and *then* you'll believe." While God does promise to hear our prayers and give us what we need if we ask Him in faith, we have to remember that what we want (a miracle) is not always what we need.

The miracles that Jesus performed weren't done in an effort to wow the crowds or to make people believe that He was God. His miracles always had a larger purpose than just a "cool trick" He pulled over nature or just to alleviate someone's personal suffering. The miracles of Christ always pointed people back to His Father and to the Kingdom of God, not to building His reputation or popularity.

As the Catechism tells us, "Moved by so much suffering Christ not only allows himself to be touched by the sick, but He makes their miseries His own, 'He took our infirmities and bore our diseases.' But He did not heal all the sick. His healings were signs of the coming of the Kingdom of God. They announced a more radical healing: the victory over sin and death through His Passover" (CCC 1505).

It's important not to fall into the trap of trying to explain away the miracles of Christ through science or sociology. Such pursuits are inconsistent with Church teaching and with the very heart of God. Christ's miracles prove not only the power God has over sin and death, but the larger reality of God's willingness to heal you and work miracles in your life, even today, in accordance with His will.

Take some time to pray through the following miracles that Jesus performed. Pay attention to the who, the what, the when, where, and how, but, as always, really ask yourself, "*Why* did Jesus do this, and how does it point me back to the Kingdom?"

REFERENCES

Joshua 24:17, Nehemiah 9:17, 1 Maccabees 15:21, Sirach 45:3, John 2:6-11, 5:5-9, 11:1-46, Matthew 8:2-4, 14:15-21, 22-33

CCC 548-554, 1335

45. THE GREATEST COMMANDMENT

We don't know his name, the guy is simply called "a lawyer," but he is famous for one reason: he had the guts to challenge Jesus, and actually ask the Lord the question everyone wanted the answer to.

You may have heard this reading before or even studied it on your own, but let's re-read it, just so we're on the same page.

"... and one of them, a lawyer, asked Him (Jesus) a question, to test Him. 'Teacher, which is the great commandment in the law?' And He said to him, 'You shall love the Lord your God with all your heart, and with all your soul, and with all your mind... and your neighbor as yourself. On these two commandments depend all the law and the prophets.'" (Matthew 22:35-40)

There have been huge books written about this passage above. Jesus calls it the greatest commandment. People call the second half "the golden rule." These verses are far too deep to do them justice here, but there are a few things that you might want to note.

First, notice that these two commandments that Jesus give us *do not* replace the Ten Commandments that God gives us. You'll see that truly loving God with heart, soul, and mind fulfills the first three of the Ten Commandments. Loving your neighbor (as yourself) properly fulfills commandments four through ten. Go back to Exodus 20 and have a look. Jesus is really efficient in His teaching, encapsulating the ten into these two.

Next, did you notice that it was a lawyer, or "scholar of the law," who challenged Jesus? Keep that in mind, it was someone who knew "the law" but not the lawmaker, he knew "the words" but not the Author. There will be many people you run into in your lifetime who might seem to know more than you about religion, but always remember: Actions follow beliefs. If someone "knows about Christ" but doesn't exude humility or love, they're like this scholar. Head knowledge doesn't always translate to a true relationship.

Lastly, don't miss what Jesus is telling them here. He's not just answering the "how to get to heaven" question. He's not giving them instructions of how to "not die" but how to *live*. Loving God and loving yourself (as God's creation) and loving your neighbor (also God's creation, even if it's difficult to see some days) is how you live life abundantly (John 10:10).

Jesus is answering this question very simply, but in a very profound way. He's saying, "Live for God today, and you'll live with God for eternity."

REFERENCES

Matthew 22:34-40, Mark 12:28-34, Luke 10:25-28

CCC 2052-2055

46. DID JESUS *REALLY* RISE FROM THE DEAD?

If He didn't, what is the point? Consider the evidence from the point of view of a scientist or lawyer — someone who is supposed to find the truth.

Jesus Christ was a real man who lived and was killed in Palestine in the early part of the first century. He is written about in sources outside of the Bible. Josephus, the Jewish historian refers to Him. The Roman historians refer to Pontius Pilate as the man who crucified Jesus so we know that Jesus was crucified.

Did He really die? If He didn't die, then He didn't really rise from the dead. Considering He was executed by professional Roman soldiers, it seems highly unlikely that Jesus would have survived. Even just being stabbed in the torso with a Roman spear would have killed anyone, since their blades were double-edged and six inches long. From all descriptions, it went through His lung and into the heart cavity where it twisted and tore the heart apart.

There were guards, both Roman and Jewish, who were placed outside of the tomb. Between the burial on Friday and the discovery of the empty tomb on Sunday morning, something happened. The Jewish leaders tried to bribe the Roman soldiers to say they had fallen asleep and the body was stolen. This obviously was not true if they needed to be paid off.

For 40 days after that Sunday, Jesus was seen by more than 500 people. He was alive. He ate and drank with them. He talked to them. However, He was different. He walked through walls and doors. At times, they did not recognize Him at first. Of all the people who saw Him, a majority of them were killed because they claimed that this Jesus of Nazareth had raised Himself from the dead. If they were lying, it is unlikely they would have died for that lie.

Do we have a photograph? No. And we don't have video. But, we do have a lot of eyewitnesses and much more evidence than we have for Bigfoot and UFOs. Maybe what we should be asking is: "What is our responsibility if the Resurrection is really true?"

REFERENCES

Matthew 22:23-31, 27:53, Luke 14:14, Acts 1:22, 2:31, Romans 6:5

CCC 639, 646

47. WHAT IS REVELATION?

Man was created in the image of God. As a result, there are things we can know about God from simply reflecting on our lives and the world around us: Being good is better then being evil, so God must be good. Beauty is better than ugliness, so God must be beautiful. Love is the greatest thing to which man can aspire to and the source of all peace in the world, so God must be love.

But we are limited. When we consider how little we can actually know about God, it is easy to see how many pagan religions came to the surface at the beginning of humankind. C. S. Lewis made the point that we are far below understanding God — like a flea trying to understand a man. The difference between God and ourselves is even more, since God is infinite and we are not.

How are we to understand this God? He must reveal Himself to us. That is the only way. There is no way we can grasp or comprehend something with our minds when that "something" created our minds!

Throughout the history of man, God has revealed Himself. The most obvious ways are through Scripture and tradition, as He makes himself known to us through a gradual unwrapping of who He is before all of mankind. When all of this comes together, we have a revealed picture of who God is. The picture is incomplete, because He is still infinite and we are not, but it is a more complete picture than what we would have without His help.

REFERENCES

1 Samuel 3:1, Psalm 119:130, Luke 2:32, Revelation 1:1

CCC 238-242, 54-67

48. HOW TRADITION WORKS

There are times when people make the suggestion that the Church "invents" traditions. This is not only impossible, but incorrect. Traditions, by their very definition, take a certain amount of time to develop. When we speak of the specific "tradition" in the Church, we must recognize how it works.

Christ conveyed a message to the apostles. After His Ascension, this message was conveyed through preaching, bearing witness, institutions, worship, and inspired writings. Through these methods, the apostles transmitted all that Christ gave them.

This tradition continues to this day. The authority of the bishops to teach this tradition is called the Magisterium. Through tradition, and the Magisterium assembled and defined the Canon of Sacred Scripture. The three elements – Scripture, tradition, and the Magisterium – work together as a three-legged table. Each leg helps the other two support, convey, and teach the faith. The other two cannot stand without the third.

When we see the three elements working together, we see the Revelation of God conveyed and transmitted to us in a way that is alive, mysterious, and part of the very Body of Christ.

REFERENCES

1 Corinthians 11:2, 2 Thessalonians 2:15, 3:6, Acts 20:35, Sirach 8:9, Matthew 15:2-6, Colossians 2:8

CCC 80-100

49. HOW TO READ AND PRAY THE SCRIPTURES

There is no "one way" to read Sacred Scripture. Some people will tell you "there is no wrong way to read the Bible." That's just stupid. If you start by reading Leviticus or 2 Chronicles, for instance, and don't know at all what the point of those books are or to whom they are written, you'll probably quit reading in less time than it took you to actually find those books in your Bible.

There may not be one way to read the Bible, but there are definitely some ways to read that will set you up for success. You want to figure out a reading plan and strategy that is going to help you build some foundations and confidence, not confuse you.

You could begin by reading Genesis all the way through to Revelation, but we would *not* suggest it... in fact, we're going to beg you not to. You see, the Bible is a "collection of books" (which is what the word *biblia* literally translates to), meaning that it was grouped together *not* to be read cover-to-cover like most novels we encounter on the shelves today, but grouped together by types of writing.

It's not that it is terrible to read the Bible from Genesis to Revelation, but it will probably confuse you because you may not understand the "bigger picture." That is not to say that you can't learn the bigger picture, but if you're just starting out without an instructor or class and are just looking to start going "deeper" on your own, it's probably better to bite off a little less.

Here's what we would suggest: Pick one book in which to start. Matthew is fine, Mark is too, though John may be a little deep to begin with. The Gospels are good because they are the actual words of Christ. The passages will be familiar to you since you've probably heard them at Sunday school, at Mass, at Life Nights, or on Retreats.

Before you read the Gospels, take some time and do a little homework. Read the introduction page to the Gospel and make some notes on specific themes to look for or facts about the audience and author. Go online to the Catholic Encyclopedia (www.newadvent. org) or work through a supplemental book, like an overview of the Bible that you can get your hands on at a Catholic bookstore. Take the time and make those notes and the text will come to life for you.

In addition, if you want a couple of other books that are easy to read, will challenge you on a daily basis, and provide some great insight and direction I'd suggest the books of **James**, **Ephesians**, **Colossians**, **Proverbs**, **Sirach**, and **Psalms**.

Remember, the only difference between the person you are now and the person you are in five years will be the people you are associated with, the choices you make, and the books that you read.

REFERENCES

Jeremiah 15:16, Romans 10:17, 2 Timothy 1:13, Hebrews 4:12-13, Mark 16:15

CCC 1437, 2653, 80-100, 101-141

*For more information on how to read the Bible and where to begin, check out the **Life Teen Catholic Teen Bible**, "Heaven's Roar" by Bob Rice, or "Ask the Bible Geek" by Mark Hart – all can be found at www.lifeteen.com in the online store.*

50. WHAT IS A SACRAMENT

The sacraments are where you encounter Jesus Christ, face to face. You don't just experience a "symbol" of Him. You don't just encounter Him in a "figurative" or "philosophical" way. No, you encounter Jesus Christ, literally. That's deep and it requires a little more information, so stick with us.

A sacrament has long been defined as "an outward sign, instituted by Christ, to bring grace." That is a concise and profound definition. Note the three components of it:

• Sacraments involve an outward sign.

• Sacraments were instituted by Jesus Christ Himself.

• Sacraments bring grace.

The sacraments were initiated and instituted by Christ. His apostles and their successors (our bishops) formally carried them out. All of the Sacraments have a Biblical basis, intrinsically, and implicitly.

The Sacraments are intimate experiences of God's grace, designed to break down all that is selfish about you, and build up Christ in you (Galatians 2:20).

One of the greatest myths and misconceptions about our Catholic faith is that the seven sacraments are not found anywhere in Scripture. Let's get right to the point: That assertion is absolutely false.

The Catholic Church is founded on Sacred Scripture *and* Sacred Tradition. The two work hand-in-hand. In fact, the need to adhere to both Scripture *and* tradition is itself, a biblical truth and Scriptural command, "Therefore, brothers, stand firm and hold fast to the traditions that you were taught, either by an oral statement or by a letter of ours" (2 Thessalonians 2:15).

Tradition gives us three different types of sacraments (in no particular order):

• Sacraments of Initiation (Baptism, Eucharist, Confirmation)

• Sacraments of Vocation (Holy Matrimony, Holy Orders)

• Sacraments of Healing (Reconciliation, Anointing)

In the next several pages, we'll spend time on each of the seven, because they are that important.

REFERENCES

Luke 5:17, 6:19, 8:46, John 16:13, 20:21-23, Matthew 16:18-19

CCC 1113-1117, 1127, 1211, 1324, 1088, 774-780

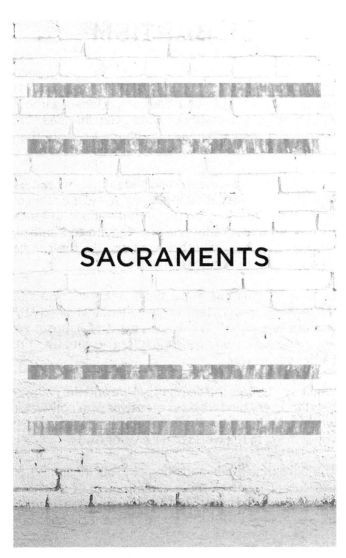

SACRAMENTS

51. BAPTISM

The earth is comprised mainly of water. Your body is comprised mainly of water. You can live longer without food than you can without water. Get the idea? We need water to live. Baptism is about a lot more than water.

Some people have the mistaken idea that the waters of Baptism are just about "washing away" the stain of original sin. Yes, they do that, but it's about so much more than that. Water is a key element to Baptism, but there are several other symbols, like the candle (light), the oil, the white garment, etc.

Baptism doesn't just erase sin; it welcomes you into the family. Through Baptism you are not "cleaned off," you are re-created. In the Sacrament of Baptism we are made new; God doesn't just forgive you, God the Father *adopts you*.

Water symbolizes the death to old life and the rising in new life. Every time we bless ourselves with holy water when we enter the Church, we renew our baptismal vows, dying to the world and living for God.

The oil signifies our anointing and our reception of the Holy Spirit. The candle reminds us to be a light to others (John 8:12) and to let Christ's light shine through us (Matthew 5:14-16). The white garment signifies our purity and sinlessness as we "put on Christ" (Galatians 3:27).

Baptism is one of the Sacraments of initiation. We baptize babies to offer them the free gift of God's grace as early as possible. If you were baptized as a child, thank your parents for ensuring you received that gift. If you'd like to learn more about Baptism in the faith so that you can be baptized, check with your parish and look into R.C.I.A.

REFERENCES

Genesis 1:1-2, 7:6-24, Psalm 51, Ezekiel 36: 25-30, Zechariah 13, Matthew 3:11,13-17, 28:18-19, Mark 1:9-11, Luke 3:16, 21-22, John 3:1-10, Acts 10:44-48, Romans 6:3-11, Hebrews 10: 19-25

CCC 1213-1284

52. EUCHARIST

Why would Jesus give us His flesh to eat? It's a good question with an even better answer.

Jesus desires to be with us in intimate, personal, simple, and humble ways (any Christian who reads the Bible, regardless of their denomination would have to agree with that). What could possibly be *simpler* than bread and wine? What could possibly be a greater example of God's *humility* than to make Himself present, known, and available through such means? What could ever be a more *personal* exchange between God and man? What could be more *intimate* than to consume Christ, to have Him actually inside of you, within you? Not even sexual intercourse is as intimate as total consumption.

Now, bearing all of these questions in mind, re-read these verses from St. John's Gospel: John 6:51-57.

The Catholic Church teaches (and always has taught) that Christ did die once and for all for the atonement of sins (Hebrews 10:11-12). Catholics are not re-sacrificing Jesus Christ. When we say it is the Eucharistic sacrifice, what we are doing is a re-presentation.

In the mind and heart of God, who is beyond space and without time (because He is just that big), each and every time we come around the altar table in our local parishes, we are, in a mystical sense, at the actual

Last Supper. Re-presenting the original sacrifice in no way necessitates a re-crucifixion.

The Mass is not just some ritual that popes and bishops made up thousands of years ago. It is the obedient response to Christ's command (Luke 22:19). In fact, from the very beginning after the Resurrection, Scripture affirms that the early Christians gathered for the Eucharist when they gathered to worship (Acts 2:42).

In addition, the *Catechism of the Catholic Church* sums up what Catholics believe quite nicely (as it always does) in sections 1366-67. Also, pray through these Scriptures: John 6:22-69, Matthew 26:1-2, 26-28, Mark 14:22-25, Luke 22:14-20, and 1 Corinthians 5:7, 10:16,11:23-29.

REFERENCES

Genesis 14:18-20, Exodus 12:1-28, Leviticus 23:4-14, Numbers 9:1-14, Deuteronomy 16:1-8, Psalm 110, Matthew 26:26-29, Mark 14:22-25, Luke 22:14-20, 24:13-43, John 6: 1-15, 23-59, Acts 2:42-43, 1 Corinthians 11:17-34

CCC 1322-1419

For more on the Scriptural roots of the Eucharist, check out "Behold the Mystery" or "Altaration" both by Mark Hart, and available in the online store at www.lifeteen. com.

53. CONFIRMATION

Confirmation is probably the most misunderstood sacrament out of the seven. Let's take a quick look at the misconceptions, shall we?

Misconception #1
Many Catholics view the Sacrament of Confirmation as a type of "graduation."

The Sacrament of Confirmation does not signify the end of your religious education or formation. Likewise, it is not the end of the parents' responsibilities either. The idea that "I just have to get my kid their sacraments" is not only a bad idea, it's bad theology. Confirmation is not an end; it's a new beginning.

Misconception #2
Some Catholics think that Confirmation is a time for the child/teen to "confirm" or "accept for themselves" what was begun at their Baptism.

Again, this is incorrect. Confirmation completes the reception of grace that was begun with the grace of Baptism. It's *not* about what *you* have to proclaim. It is about the Church confirming what happened to you at Baptism and saying that you are ready to receive the Holy Spirit in this manner.

Misconception #3
Some think that a sponsor has to be a relative or the godparent.

Sometimes, well-intentioned parents insist on who your sponsor "should be." Their input is great and should always be respected, but the decision is yours. Just because you were named after "Great Aunt Agatha," or because "cousin Hector" hasn't gotten to be a sponsor yet doesn't mean they are spiritually prepared for the duty. The sponsor should not only be a confirmed Catholic who goes to Mass every week, but an example of what it means to *live the faith*. It doesn't have to be your godparent or even a family member. Find someone you respect in the faith, in or out of your family tree, and prayerfully consider them.

As for Great Aunt Agatha, you can always invite her to the Rite of Confirmation Mass to see you receive the Sacrament. Oh, and tell her to get there early, it'll probably be crowded.

REFERENCES

Exodus 19:16-19, Leviticus 23:15-22, Numbers 28:26-31, Joel 3:1-5, Luke 3:16, Acts 2:1-12, 8:14–17, 9:17, 19:6, 1 Corinthians 12-14, Romans 8:1-13, Hebrews 6:1-2

CCC 1285-1321

For more information on Confirmation, check out the "One8 Sponsor Handbook" and "Gifted" by Alison Griswold found at www.lifeteen.com in the online store.

54. RECONCILIATION

Sin has a way of blinding and deafening us to the face and the voice of God. Sin becomes suffocating and, in time, addicting. Sin works in a cycle: It starts with something small and continues to build off of itself into something large. Eventually it grows so large it seems there is no use fighting it and no turning back. Here's one analogy of how it works:

"I went to get my car washed a few weeks back. Every time I go, it's the same old story: My car stays clean for a few days, then it's dirty again. You know the drill. When your car is clean, you're much more careful where and how you drive. Speaking personally, after a car wash I pay much closer attention on the road. I go out of my way to avoid puddles, dirt, or anything else that could potentially splash up and destroy my recently washed vehicle. However, the minute I get some dirt on my car all bets are off. I'm driving through construction zones, purposely hitting puddles and 'off-roading.' I think to myself, 'Well, self, *it's already dirty, so what does it matter?*'

I am the same way when it comes to Reconciliation.

When I leave the church after Confession, I am so much more conscious about everything. I become more conscious about my language, my thoughts, the way I act, etc. After a good Confession, sin is like a mud puddle... I try to avoid it, to keep my car (soul) pristine.

Once I sin, though, I keep on sinning... sometimes even looking for opportunities to sin (you know, since I'm already "dirty).

The problem is that it is the wrong way of thinking on my part. God would rather have me at the 'car wash of the soul' (Reconciliation) every day, than be out there on the streets in a 'dirty car' — not in a state of grace.

When it comes to addictive sinful behavior, especially like pornography or masturbation, those puddles get even more difficult to avoid. When we surround ourselves with porn (or the temptation of porn), it's like putting puddles on every street we'd drive down... sinning becomes almost impossible to avoid."[3]

As we've already discussed in this book, sin destroys your capacity to love and to receive love. In addition, no sin is private. Every sin, no matter how public or how private it may seem, affects other people, the whole body of Christ.

If your car is maybe a little dirtier and muddier right now than it should be, (and we've all been there from time to time) get to the car wash! Start fresh. Start clean. The grace that comes from Reconciliation helps to make us more aware of the mud puddles in our lives, strengthens us to avoid them, and convicts us to take another route where the streets are cleaner.

REFERENCES

Matthew 9:2-8, 16:19, 18:15-18, John 20: 21-23, 2 Corinthians 5:17-20, James 5: 16-19, 1 John 1: 8-2:2, 2 Samuel 12: 1-13, Psalms 32 and 51, Isaiah 22: 21-22

CCC 1420-1498

For more on Reconciliation and its Scriptural roots check out www.lifeteen.com or pick up a copy of "Come Clean" and "Ask the Bible Geek."

55. ANOINTING
OF THE SICK

If Confirmation is the most misunderstood sacrament, than Anointing of the Sick might be the most underused. It's a popular misconception that you call for anointing when all hope is gone. It's the idea that when the doctors can't do anything else, it's time to let the priest say a "goodbye" prayer.

Many Catholics live their lives praying that they'd be given "just enough warning" to receive Anointing of the Sick on their deathbed, like some kind of Willy Wonka-esque golden ticket into heaven.

While the Sacrament absolutely remits all sins in such a situation, it is far more than that.

The Anointing of the Sick is not reserved for the deathbed. It is a gift for your life. It offers hope and healing. It offers comfort to those who are worn down or fatigued by illness. To be clear, you don't go running up to the church asking for the Sacrament if you have a cold or the flu. It is for more serious times, like prior to an operation or procedure, after enduring a long bout of illness, or when the situation is particularly painful or grave. The anointing of the sick is yet another opportunity to encounter Christ and His healing touch.

The grace of the Sacrament is not a miracle pill. It does not necessarily heal all physical or terminal afflictions. That's not why the Sacrament exists. It's not a lucky rabbit's foot of healing. That being said, it has been known to work miraculously in some cases. As with anything else in life, it's about God's will.

The Scriptures show us that Jesus has a heart for the sick and the infirmed (Mark 6:2, Matthew 10:8). They also tell us that we ought to anoint one another, lay hands on one another, and pray for healing (James 5:14-15).

REFERENCES

Isaiah 1:6, Mark 6:12-13, 16:17-18, Luke 10:29-37, James 5:13-15

CCC 1499-1532

56. HOLY MATRIMONY

Marriage was instituted by God at Creation and blessed by Jesus Christ at the Wedding at Cana. In all things there is the "form," how something appears, and the "substance," what that thing really is.

Marriage is the same way. Since all Sacraments are an earthly sign of the grace that God gives us to live with Him in Heaven, we know that there is something more than what we see as a couple recites their vows.

In their wedding vows, a couple freely promises to give themselves to each other totally and faithfully for the rest of their lives, and be open to the life that may come from the relationship.

A marriage in the Church is not complete until the couple has consummated it in sexual intercourse. Intercourse is the physical representation of their vows — freely choosing to love each other in a way that is completely total, faithful, and will bear new life. These are earthly signs of what is happening on the spiritual level.

Two souls become one. There is the possibility that their love is so deep that another soul will be born. The two souls are not two "but one" and they will be bound together for all eternity. This is why the Catholic Church cannot grant divorces. It is not within the power of the Church to separate what has been joined by God.

An annulment is a different matter. In an annulment, the Church declares that there was a barrier that kept the couple from entering into a true marriage at the beginning and so the marriage was not truly binding.

The Church needs good marriages in the same way that she needs good priests, brothers, and sisters. This should constantly be in our prayers.

REFERENCES

Genesis 2:21-24, Deuteronomy 24:1-5, Mark 10:1-12, Matthew 19:1-12, 1 Thessalonians 4:3-8, Colossians 3:18-19, 1 Corinthians 7:1-16, 1 Peter 3:1-7

CCC 1601-1666

57. HOLY ORDERS

Since there are two vocations, (marriage and celibacy) the celibate vocation has its own Sacrament. The Sacrament of Holy Orders gives a man the ability to participate in the Church in the person of Christ, becoming Christ for the Church so that He may remain with us forever.

The first level of Holy Orders is the Deaconate. There are two types of Deacons, the Transitional, and the Permanent. The Transitional Deaconate is the temporary state where a man takes the vows of obedience and celibacy and serves the Church in the Liturgy of the Word and assisting in the charitable work of the Body of Christ. The Permanent Deacon also assists in this area, but may be married while the Transitional Deacon will eventually move on to the priesthood.

Priests are extensions of the bishop who is responsible for the diocese. The priest functions in a way as the hands, feet, eyes, and ears of the bishop among the people. He helps by transmitting the guidance of the bishop for the diocese and in administering the sacraments. While the priest may administer the sacraments, he is a servant of the people in the parish and obedient to the service of the bishop in the diocese.

The last level of Holy Orders is that of bishop. The bishop is a direct descendent of the apostles, serving the Church by passing on the teachings of Jesus to the people. Archbishops are also bishops. They have all the same responsibilities but serve a different region/jurisdiction. A cardinal is a bishop or archbishop of a higher rank with special responsibilities and jurisdictions.

It is through the bishop that we realize our contact directly to Jesus and what He taught to the apostles. If we go back through the generations, we will eventually find a bishop who was blessed and anointed for his mission by Christ Himself.

REFERENCES

Genesis 15:18-20, Leviticus 8: 1-13, Deuteronomy 18:1-8, Acts 6:1-6, Hebrews 9:6-7, 10:12-14, 1 Timothy 3:1-13, 5:17-23, 2 Timothy 4:5, 2 Corinthians 3:6, 11:23, Ephesians 3:7, Titus 1:5-9, 1 Peter 2:9-10, James 5:14-15

CCC 1533-1600

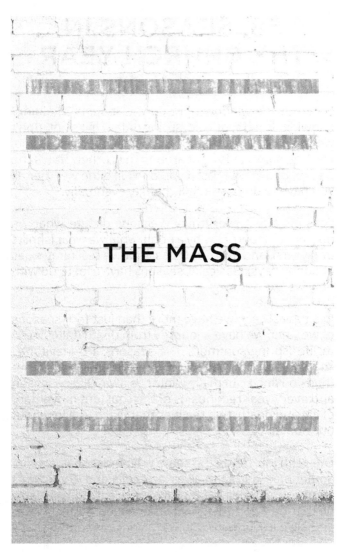

THE MASS

58. SEASONS IN THE CHURCH YEAR

Look out the window right now. Is it sunny? Raining? Snowing? Is it hot or cold, spring or fall? If it's hot, don't worry it will be soon cooling off. If it's freezing outside, fret not, summer is right around the corner. That's the beauty of the seasons; if you don't like the weather all you have to do is wait. It'll change, eventually.

Seasons affect everything. Seasons dictate what we do (shovel snow or lay by a pool), what we wear (shorts or sweats), and even, at times, how we feel (gray skies or sunny days). Basically, seasons have a lot to do with how we live our lives.

In a typical year, we have more than just four seasons of weather, we have a journey from death (fall/winter) to life (spring/summer). The seasons are inevitable. You and I cannot stop summer from coming any more than you and I can make winter go away. Every season and every year reminds us of the constant movement of life and death, two realities that teach us a lot about our humanity.

Our faith journey is the same way; it has seasons too. Sometimes our faith lives are cold and sometimes warm, sometimes we feel like we are dead spiritually or that our world is gray. Other times we feel warm and alive in our faith and our outlook is sunny. That's the way life works: There is death and there is life, literally and figuratively, every day and every year.

Our Church has seasons too, liturgical seasons. Why you may ask? Well it's not to mirror the secular seasons. Our Church has seasons to walk us through our own spiritual journey, from death to life, each year. If we walk with our Lord through the liturgical seasons each year we will grow in our faith, as it deepens with every season.

The Church's liturgical year begins with the season of Advent. Following Advent we have Christmas, Lent, Easter, and Ordinary Time. You'll note the different seasons within the Church calendar in a number of ways. First, pay attention to colors. The priest (and probably the whole church) will reflect what season you are in. If it's Lent, for instance, you'll see a lot of purple, the color of penitence. If it's Ordinary Time you'll see green, Pentecost or martyr's feast days will bring out red, Easter will be white. You get the idea. Usually the music and the prayers will change too.

The Church doesn't do this just to keep things fresh, but to signal all of our senses to where we are on the spiritual journey. The seasons are a great way to draw us into our faith journeys more. So, this Sunday, pay attention to the season and ask yourself (or someone around you), "What does this have to do with our journey to Christ today?"

"Either we live the liturgical year with its varying seasons of joy and sorrow, work and rest, or we follow the pattern of the world." – Helen McLoughlin

REFERENCES

Ecclesiastes 3, Psalm 104:27, Deuteronomy 28:12, Jeremiah 5:24, Daniel 7:12, Galatians 6:9

CCC 1163-1178

59. MUSIC IN THE CHURCH

Music has been around longer than Christianity. The Church actually considers it a "treasure... greater even than that of any other art."[4] This is because music has always played a part in the liturgy of every time period and community.

The Psalms were sung with musical instruments during the Jewish liturgies. The Church adopted this tradition and continued to develop it. In our Catholic liturgy, the music should serve as the soundtrack to a movie, fitting with the action, words, and what is taking place. Many times, when we walk out of a Mass and the action or the music did not fit, we may comment on it. However, we must realize that the liturgy and all its components are difficult to execute and require prayer, preparation, and participation.

Music is designed for us to participate in. It is meant to be a meditation that moves and lifts us toward God. It should be beautiful, reflecting the beauty of God. It should have the participation of the entire community, much as we as Catholics are in communion. It should give the respect to the liturgy that it deserves. The words of the music should always reflect the doctrine of the Church and the culture of the people who are celebrating the liturgy. It should also bring the community to more active participation in prayer.

This means that the hymns we sing at Mass are meant for our participation. Each one is a prayer, so when we sit back and opt out of song we also are missing out on rich prayer. Music is an emotive experience and is a major part of the human existence. This is no mistake; God designed us this way. There are plenty of places where we misuse this gift and do not glorify God with our music. Liturgy is a place where the natural desire to create music and express ourselves through it can be lived out to the glory of God. We use music to express our prayer in a way that sometimes words alone cannot express. It has been said that when a person sings, he or she prayers twice. No place is this more true than when we sing in the liturgy.

REFERENCES

1 Corinthians 14:15, Colossians 3:16, Ephesians 5:19, Tobit 13:18,1 Maccabees 4:24, 2 Maccabees 1:30, Psalm 9:3, Acts 16:25

CCC 1156

60. CATHOLIC CROSSFIT: STAND, SIT, AND KNEEL

Have you ever been driving or riding in a car and accidentally cut someone off? Perhaps you didn't check the mirror or were talking on the phone or texting (that's dangerous, by the way). Usually the person that you cut off is less than enthused. They might hit the horn, speed up and stare or, worse yet, practice some "sign language."

If you've ever been on the receiving end of the middle finger, you know how it makes you feel. It's so random isn't it? A person takes one of the fingers on their hand and simply raises it and your peace is shattered. That gesture makes a huge statement. Little issues become big issues all from the extension of one pudgy, little digit. We communicate with our bodies. Exterior expressions and gestures say a lot about our interior thoughts and feelings. In a similar but obviously less offensive way, we can use our hands and bodies to communicate in prayer and in worship as well.

Kneeling, for instance, is a common sign of humility and respect but is far more than an action. Often at Mass we might just kneel because everyone else is kneeling and we want to be consistent. The reality is that our kneeling should be an external expression of the posture of our heart. When we fall on our knees it is a silent, but visible statement about what is transpiring and about whom we are worshipping.

You'll find at other times during the Mass we sit or stand. Standing is seen in a light of urgency and preparedness. At the time for the Gospel acclamation we stand, ready and willing to receive Christ's words. We're not saying that the other readings that preceded the Gospel aren't important, only that the Gospel holds an even greater importance.

Our posture changes depending upon what we are doing during specific parts of the Mass. It should not be seen in comparison, like "this part is more important than that part" since the entire liturgy is important. Rather it should signal to us to focus and help us stay attentive to what is happening at all times.

Always consider what you are saying intentionally, unintentionally, verbally, or nonverbally by your body language. If you are sitting in the pew with your arms crossed and a nasty look on your face, it communicates something doesn't it? Even if you don't mean to look angry or bored, your body language says something different. You don't have to be in traffic to hinder someone else's faith walk. Be conscious of what your body is saying in action (and in dress). Self-awareness is the foundation of true holiness.

REFERENCES

Psalm 95:6, Philippians 2:10-11, Matthew 9:18, Luke 22:41, Malachi 3:2, Acts 10:26, Ephesians 6:14

GIRM 42-44

For more information on the Mass, check out "Behold the Mystery" by Mark Hart found at www.lifeteen.com in the online store.

61. VESTMENTS: WHY ALL THE ROBES?

"Why is that dude wearing a dress?" I was asked by an inquisitive teenager. He wasn't trying to be disrespectful. He was trying to figure out why the priest wears vestments. William was new to the Catholic faith, coming along to a fall kickoff for our Life Teen program. I'll never forget that moment. The question was so raw and honest. He was intrigued. I think of it every time I see William now... only now I call him Father William and he's the one "wearing a dress."

There are two robes worn by the priest at Mass actually: the alb and the chasuble. There is also a stole, the fabric that goes around the neck and drapes to the floor, but that's a different thing. We'll just focus on the robes for now.

The chasuble is the external garment worn by the priest. The color for the chasuble and stole depends on the liturgical season (Advent, Lent, Easter, Ordinary Time). Sometimes the chasuble, the stole, or both have ornate designs that represent special feasts, saints, or themes.

The alb, derived from "albus" (the Latin word for white) has been in common use as a liturgical garment since the latter part of the fourth century. The original symbolism was a direct reference to the seamless white garment that Christ wore during His Passion.

It has always been used to remind the liturgical celebrant that his role at that moment is *in persona Christi* (the person of Christ). By simply covering his daily clothing with the white garment, the vestment is (and should be) a constant reminder to the priest that he is no longer acting on or in his own accord, for "it is no longer I, but Christ who lives in me" (Galatians 2:20).

Now, want to know something very interesting and quite cool?

For many centuries, the vesting ritual that the celebrant goes through prior to a liturgy has been very precise. Each garment carries with it a spoken prayer. The particular prayer for the alb was one that reminded the priest to put away whatever worldly cares or worries he was carrying with him so he would be enabled to meet the spiritual needs of his congregation, and allowing him to become *tabula rasa* (a blank slate), on which the prayers and intentions of his congregation could be written.

Next time you see your priest in the alb, stop and say a prayer of thanksgiving for his vocation, his response, and for the priesthood. For, it is the Priesthood of Jesus Christ.

REFERENCES

Genesis 37:3, Leviticus 16:4, 1 Samuel 17:38, Matthew 5:40, Luke 6:29, John 19:23, 2 Kings 2:12, Job 29:14, Baruch 4:20, Zechariah 8:23, Malachi 2:16, Matthew 22:11, Jude 1:23, Revelation 19:8

CCC 1142, 1539-1545, 1554, 1572-1574, 1095, 1168

62. COMMUNION

When you hear the word "communion," you probably think of rising from your pew during Mass and walking forward to receive the Eucharist. Certainly, that is communion. In truth, though, communion is *that and a whole lot more.* It's not just the "action" of going forward to receive Jesus in His precious Body and Blood, but truly becoming *one with* God.

The dictionary defines communion as "an exchange of intimate thoughts and feelings." And while the good folks at Webster do a nice job, that isn't nearly deep enough. Communion in Christ is more than "sharing common feelings" and more than expressing "intimate feelings." True communion in Christ is an exchange of self.

It is the Holy Spirit who brings us into communion with Christ, since it is only by the Holy Spirit that we can even proclaim that Christ is Lord (1 Corinthians 12:3)! The same way that Christ leads us into a more intimate relationship (and exchange of self) with God the Father, the Holy Spirit leads us into a more intimate relationship with Christ.

In addition, we are called to be in communion not only with Christ, but with His greater body, the Church. The Latin root word for communion, *communio*, means "common;" we are bound together with the greater body of Christ, a body of believers with whom we have common beliefs and share common realities. One of the "realities" that we share is that God is God and we are not; God is the Creator, we are His creation.

At Holy Mass we come together, in community (same root word), and enter into physical and spiritual "communion" with one another and with God. At that same time, we are surrounded by all of the saints and angels (Hebrews 12:1), in communion with the mystical body of Christ who have gone before us. In God's timelessness, we are worshipping alongside the heavenly host, during this re-presentation of Christ's once-and-for-all perfect sacrifice, in perfect communion. Then, during the Mass, we receive communion (Christ's true presence) in order that we might become saints, ourselves!

Take a minute and ponder that. In fact, go before the Blessed Sacrament and ask the Lord to reveal to you the beautiful simplicity, yet complexity, of *communion.*

REFERENCES

1 Corinthians 10:16, Ephesians 4:12, Psalm 104:13-15, Genesis 14:18, Deuteronomy 8:3, Acts 2:42, Luke 4:4, John 6:22-59, Romans 7:4

CCC 725, 1650, 1244, 1384-1387, 1333-1335, 790, 1126, 1533-1536, 2565

63. TRANSUBSTANTIATION EXPLAINED

We Catholics love big words: epiclesis, doxology, catechesis, Magisterium. Perhaps no word is more important and more misunderstood than transubstantiation.

Transubstantiation is the term used to describe what literally happens at every Catholic Mass, through the power of the Holy Spirit working through the Sacramental priesthood of Jesus Christ. Transubstantiation is when the gifts of bread and wine are *substantially* changed (transubstantiated *not* transformed) into the real flesh and blood of Jesus Christ. The Catholic Church at the Council of Trent summarized transubstantiation quite nicely. To read more about it, check out your Catechism (CCC 1376-77).

Many Christians (and some Catholics unfortunately) have a difficult time with this teaching because it does not "appear" that the bread and wine change. So, how do we as Catholics explain our belief in the Real Presence, if the bread and the wine still look like simple bread and wine? Think about it, it would be a lot easier if all of the sudden the bread oozed blood or if we used clear glasses and white wine turned into red wine, right?

Well, it's complicated to do in a small amount of space, but let's give it a try.

There are two "levels" that make up an object: the accidents and the substance. The accidents are the appearance, taste, look, and feel of an object, but the substance is what it really is. Take a chair; it has accidents and substance. Say that you saw the chair in several pieces and then take those pieces of wood and reconfigure them with nails to make a coffee table. You've changed the *accidents* of the chair into a table, but the *substance* of the chair has not been changed, it's still made up of wood molecules. Make sense? So, at Mass the *accidents* of the bread and wine do not change, but through the power of the Holy Spirit, the *substance* of the bread and wine are altered into Christ's body and blood on the altar.

The Eucharist is not a mystery to be solved but a mystery to behold. The gifts are not transformed but *transubstantiated*. This miracle turns you into a walking tabernacle, literally changing you from the inside out. This uniquely intimate expression of God's grace, through Holy Communion, has a power to transform and "transubstantiate" us like nothing else on earth.

REFERENCES

Matthew 18:20, 26:26, Romans 8:34, 12:5, 1 Corinthians 11:24, Luke 22:19, Mark 14:22

CCC 1373-1377, 1404, 1413

64. WHY CAN'T NON-CATHOLICS RECEIVE THE EUCHARIST?

Catholics believe that the Eucharist is truly the divine flesh of Jesus, not a piece of bread representing Him, not a symbol of Him, but *truly* Him. Non-Catholics do not believe this fact. On the most fundamental level, that is why non-Catholics who attend a Catholic Mass cannot receive. It is less about their "worthiness" and more about not putting them in a position to denounce their own beliefs.

Other faiths have "bread and wine" at their services... we don't. We have the actual Body and Blood of Jesus Christ present in the Eucharist, under the form of bread and wine. Most of the other faiths you're probably thinking believe that the bread and wine are simply reenactments or remembrances of the actions of the Last Supper, but the Church's teaching goes so much deeper in our belief in the Real Presence of Christ in the Eucharist.

Read Luke 22:19, it's that part about "This is my body" that I'd like you to notice. We believe that He whom we receive is truly Jesus Christ. In asking a non-Catholic to receive the Eucharist you are asking them to either deny their own religion and become Catholic or you're saying that you don't really believe in the Real Presence of Christ, either way... it's not too good.

There is nothing wrong with wanting your friends to feel welcome at Mass, but this can be done without compromising our beliefs. Most Dioceses have guidelines for what non-Catholics can do during Communion and at almost all the Life Teen Masses I've been to, the priest gives those instructions at the beginning of Communion. We want people to feel welcome in our parishes, but we also have to remain true to the fact that there are differences in our religious practices. We are not like "other churches," we are the Catholic Church and proud of it.

I often invite my friends from other religious backgrounds to Mass. I always take the time to explain to them that at Communion they can receive a blessing or simply pray from their pew. Never have any of them been insulted or offended. They expect it in most cases and sometimes the reverence they see in the Catholics who are receiving starts them on the road to their own conversion of faith and leads them back to the Church.

Put simply, non-Catholics can't receive the Eucharist out of mutual respect. In addition, most Christians might be surprised to learn that the Bible says it is a no-no too. St. Paul warned people about going forward to receive the true flesh and blood of Christ if they did not believe it to be so (1 Corinthians 11:23-29).

REFERENCES

1 Corinthians 11:23-29, 12:13, John 6:22-59, Acts 2:42

CCC 1398, 1374, 1322, 1212, 790, 100

For more information on the Mass, check out "Behold the Mystery" by Mark Hart found at www.lifeteen.com in the online store.

65. WORSHIP: THE WHY, HOW, AND WHO

Worship as defined by the Catechism is "Adoration and honor given to God, which is the first act of the virtue of religion." If we are to honor and adore God, we would worship.

Traditionally, the Church depicted worship as something done at Mass, during the Liturgy of the Hours, or while reading the Scriptures. As such, worship was reserved for the select few clergy and religious who made it a career.

Today, worship has taken on a number of forms. Through contemporary music, prayer services, and Eucharistic Adoration, we are able to adore and honor God in many different ways.

We honor God whenever we give Him the credit that is due to Him. In the same way that we would give credit to someone in history for something he or she accomplished, we do the same for God. Since God created the entire world, it is important to remember that all honor truly goes to Him.

When we adore God, we place ourselves in His presence and recognize His glory. Recognizing that one is our Creator is something that goes beyond time and space. Placing ourselves in adoration of God can be a time of tremendous healing, spiritual guidance, and peace.

So, there is really no difference between traditional and modern worship except the boundaries in which we place it. Someone may prefer traditional worship, while someone else may prefer modern worship. When we get caught up in which is better, we lose the focus on adoring and worshipping God. Period.

REFERENCES

1 Corinthians 14:15, 1 Chronicles 15:27-28, Romans 15:9, Revelation 14:3, Acts 16:25, 1 Thessalonians 5:16-17, Ephesians 5:19

CCC 2097, 2184-2187, 1179, 1121-1123, 2136

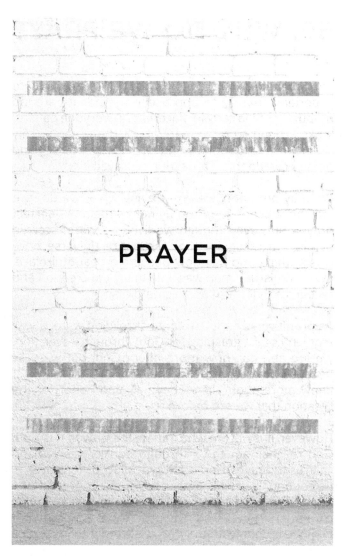

PRAYER

66. WHY DO WE PRAY?

The world around us is beautiful. We only need to experience nature to appreciate the beauty around us, but there is a certain place where everyone pauses, looks around, and wonders about the Creator. Only those with minds and hearts for seeking diversity and beauty can do this. This action is prayer.

We may not know we are praying when we do it. It may be subconscious. It may not be the most perfect prayer, but, even though we live in a world scarred by sin, we recognize that the entire universe once was nothing and has now become a beautiful place. Even prehistoric man was able to look at creation and recognize that there was a creator.

As primitive as early attempts at religion were, it was mankind's first grasping for God. Through Revelation, we are able to know more about God, but we pray because we recognize that there is a Creator we must know more about, love above all, and honor for the creation that we see before us.

However, it is not we who initiate the prayer. It is God. God reaches out to us through our very selves and calls us to prayer. God is always calling us to prayer — he continually invites and waits for our conversation. Really, this is the heart of prayer. It is our line of communication to God. The best relationships involve heavy communication – our relationship with God is no different. Prayer allows us to not only speak to God, but it forms our heart to be attentive to the ways that God responds to us. Prayer changes our relationship with God because it allows God to change who we are. It is a vital part of our walk with the Lord; after all, you probably wouldn't go longer than a day or so without speaking to your best friend. Our friendship with God is no different.

REFERENCES

John 4:10, 7:37-39, Genesis 24:45, Matthew 6:9-15, Jeremiah 29:12, James 4:8-9, Romans 6:5, Ephesians 3:18-21, Numbers 21:3, 1 Samuel 1:12-16, Luke 8:9-14

CCC 2558-2865

For more information on the why and how of prayer, check out "Come Pray" found at www.lifeteen.com in the online store.

67. WHAT IS PRAYER?

Whenever we contemplate God, we pray. This means that we think about God and we feel His presence. Whenever we do this in a way that is the will of God, we are praying. When we are able to recognize that it is God who calls us to prayer, we are able to humbly think about and love God.

People pray in many different ways. What makes a prayer distinctly Christian? Let's put it this way, if you were in a relationship with someone, you would need to talk with him or her regularly for that relationship to function, grow, and thrive. Most of the time, if someone does not want to be in a relationship, he or she will refuse to talk to the significant other.

Prayer is the same way. We need to talk to God. We need to talk to God in such a way that builds our relationship with Him. If we do not do that, our relationship with Him will suffer and fall apart on our end. Of course, it won't fall apart on God's end, as He is always talking to us.

God is infinitely Good, and that infinite Goodness created us. Prayer is keeping ourselves in relationship with that Good, His son, Jesus Christ. Jesus also promised that the Holy Spirit would be with us always until the end of time. When we pray in the silence of our hearts, we build our relationship with the Holy Spirit.

REFERENCES

Matthew 6:9-15, Luke 18:9-14, Romans 8:26, Psalm 130:1, Jeremiah 29:12, James 4:8-9, Nehemiah 1:6-11, Tobit 3:11-16, Job 42:8, Isaiah 12:3

CCC 2559-2597

68. DIFFERENT FORMS OF PRAYER: AN INTRODUCTION

There are very few times I will pass up an all-you-can-eat buffet. I like variety and when I sit down to a meal of a little bit of everything, I just get the feeling that, at the very least, I'm thorough. Prayer is like that. We have a veritable all you can eat buffet of prayer available to us in the Catholic tradition. Make no mistake, the source and summit of the faith, the highest form of prayer that we are able to take part in is the Holy Mass, the re-presentation (not "re-sacrifice") of Christ's Passion. No other form of prayer allows us to literally consume Christ's flesh. That being said, however, prayer is an ascent of the heart, mind, and the soul to God.

Prayer can be expressed in a number of different ways. There is prayer that is vocal, there is prayer that is considered meditative, and there is contemplative prayer. When we pray, we jump into the arms of a loving Father and allow Him to talk to us, to hold us and to love us.

The Our Father is the perfect form of *vocal prayer.* Vocal prayer takes what is in our hearts and expresses it through our body. Just as someone who speaks in sign language speaks with his or her body, we do as well when we make the Sign of the Cross, open our hands, and kneel. Many types of vocal prayer are formal, but it can also be informal — a vocalization of what is on the inside.

Meditation is reflecting on God, mostly in the Scriptures, and using our very beings to engage with God and strengthen the theological virtues of faith, hope, and love. Our beings include our emotions, intellect, will, imagination, and desires.

Contemplative prayer is when we simply bask in the love of God, the way a sunbather basks in sunshine. There is only silence. The only presence is the divine love of God in perfect love. It is like being with a friend with whom you don't need to say anything to share what you are feeling — merely being with the person is enough.

In the following pages, we'll be discussing several different prayer practices in more depth. Before we go there, it's useful to learn more about what forms of prayer we will be discussing.

The *Catechism of the Catholic Church* discusses the following five types of prayer in detail:

Blessing and Adoration – *CCC* 2626-2628
Prayer of Petition – *CCC* 2629-2633
Prayer of Intercession – *CCC* 2634-2636
Prayer of Thanksgiving – *CCC* 2637-2638
Prayer of Praise – *CCC* 2639-2643

Take some time to read through each form. Familiarize yourself with what makes them different. Then take some time to actually pray. Reading about prayer is wonderful, but it can never take the place of prayer itself. Don't fall into the trap of saying, "I have to pray more." Go ahead and do it. There's no time like the present. God is always available.

REFERENCES

Luke 11:2-4, Matthew 6:9-13

For more in-depth guidance and explanation of prayer and its different forms, check out "Come Pray" from the online store at www.lifeteen.com.

69. THE ROSARY

The rosary is the most famous and most popular *chaplet* that we have as Catholics. A chaplet is a prayer devotion that commonly utilizes beads. It comes from a French word for "wreath" or "crown." While the structure and devotion of the rosary has its roots with the "desert fathers," it is **St. Dominic** who is historically credited with giving the structured gift of the rosary to the greater Church.

When we pray the rosary we meditate on the life of Christ, gazing upon Him through the lens and window of Mary's soul. Since she is our Blessed Mother, gifted to us from His cross **(John 19:27)**, it makes perfect sense that we would seek to look upon Christ in such an intimate and sinless way, as she does. The rosary draws us into more perfect discipleship, and focuses our prayer on the Trinity.

The rosary was originally developed as a way to teach the life of Christ and Mary to those who were not able to read, and to assist those (who were not clergy) in praying the Liturgy of the Hours, the prayer of the Church. Through the rosary, we take our intentions to Mary and show our honor and respect for her as the greatest of all the saints and an example to us all.

It might be difficult for you to pray the rosary, because of the repetition of the prayers. I'll be honest with you, even though I pray it daily, it can still be tough for me sometimes. Repetition can have a soothing effect. The rhythm can be both a good thing and a bad thing (if you're like me). I have to work very hard to stay focused. Kneeling helps. That being said, it is a great gift. All prayer is directed to the Father, through Jesus Christ.

The Rosary is directed to Christ, guided by His mother. We should be thankful for the guided, Scriptural prayers (the Our Father, Hail Mary, Glory Be), always. They help us pray. At times they are all I can verbalize, when I'm too tired, distracted or too much in pain to muster anything else, of my own. And remember, we must always keep in mind Jesus' warning not to let our prayers become repetitious babbling or empty phrases (Matthew 6:7). Sometimes it helps to recite the prayers more slowly, to ensure we are *praying and not just saying the prayers.*

To learn HOW to pray the rosary, the order and the prayers, turn to the Appendix, pgs 277-279.

70. LECTIO DIVINA

Lectio Divina ("Divine Reading" for everyone keeping score on our Latin to English translation score card) is an incredible form of prayer in which you more deeply encounter God through His Word. More than just a program on how to read the Bible, it is a prayerful process in which you literally put yourself into the story, making yourself available to hear God speaking to your soul. The more you try it, the more you'll experience the Word of God come to life *in your life* in all new ways.

There are four steps to the *Lectio Divina: lectio, meditatio, oratio, and contemplatio.* Or in English they are: reading, meditating, speaking, and contemplating.

As you begin, you should pick a passage from Scripture. For starters, try to select one that is not too long and not dependent on surrounding stories for understanding. A few you might want to try would be Jesus' Baptism (Mark 1:9-11), the call of the disciples (Matthew 4:18-22), or the teaching about the greatest commandment (Luke 10:25-28).

Enter into a prayerful environment and space. Silence yourself. Ask the Holy Spirit to fall upon you and burn within you, opening your eyes and ears in a new way.

Step One – *Lectio (Read)*

Read the Scripture passage slowly and intentionally, listening as if God is speaking it directly to you, because He is doing just that. What are the main points, characters, and details of the passage?

Step Two – *Meditatio (Meditate)*

What is the word or phrase that really jumps out at you or that spoke to you in this passage? What impact do these words have on your soul this day?

Step Three – *Oratio (Speak)*

Have a conversation with God about what you've read, what you do and don't understand, what jumped out at you during your meditation time (step two). Ask God how it might be calling you to change your life and faith walk.

Step Four – *Contemplatio (Contemplate)*

The final step is less about you and more about God. Simply take some time to be with God. Bring no agenda, list of petitions or questions, simply be with Him and allow Him to be with you. What is He saying to you now?

If you can commit these four steps to memory and keep practicing *Lectio Divina*, you'll be amazed how quickly you begin to grow in knowledge and in holiness. You'll also be surprised at how much more you want to read the Scriptures.

REFERENCES

Jeremiah 15:16, Luke 4:4, Acts 2:42, Philippians 3:8, John 4:14, 17:7

CCC 2705-08, 2763-2774, 1177

For a guided reflection of the Gospel of Mark, check out "Heaven's Roar" by Bob Rice found at www.lifeteen.com in the online store.

71. NOVENAS

A novena is a nine-day prayer devotion, public or private, in the Catholic Church to obtain special graces. The name "novena" comes from the Latin word *novem* which means "nine."

Now, you might be wondering, "Why nine? That's kind of random, isn't it?" Well, yes and no. Nine can be a number symbolic of expectancy and preparation. For example, how many months is a woman pregnant for? In the case of a novena, there were nine days between Jesus' Ascension and the Spirit's descent at Pentecost. During those nine days, Mary and the apostles were instructed to pray, preparing to receive the Holy Spirit on that feast day.

Novenas are powerful expressions and exercises in prayer. There are special devotions at your disposal for special causes. The regularity and consistency of a novena, for nine straight days, develops virtuous habits of faithfulness and discipline in your prayer life. In addition, it's a great way to tap into one of the greatest gifts of God to His children which is the Church, the body of Christ, the communion of saints. When you invite the saints to pray with you and for you, you are uniting yourself to the mystical body of Christ in a whole new way.

Just to be clear, novenas are always offered to Christ. Even if it is a novena with a specific saint, don't misunderstand the direction your prayers are going. When you offer a novena to St. Therese, for instance, your prayers are not *ending* with St. Therese, you're asking her to *join* her prayers to yours (for nine days), as you offer them (and she personally "walks them") to our Savior, Jesus Christ.

If you've never prayed a novena, get yourself a book of prayers or go online and find one. There are countless specific novenas for Jesus, the Holy Spirit, our Blessed Mother, St. Joseph and just about any popular saint you can think of. Read up on them. Print one out and give it a try.

God's grace is waiting...

REFERENCES

Acts 1-2, 1 Thessalonians 5:17

CCC 2634-47, 2683-84

72. ADORATION

The Bible is a book of promises. There are over 4,000 promises in it, all given by God to His children, to you. One of those promises came from Jesus as He ascended into heaven, following His Resurrection.

"Go therefore and make disciples of all nations... and lo, I am with you always, to the close of the age."(Matthew 28:19-20)

Jesus did not mean this figuratively or (merely) spiritually. No, Jesus promised to stay with us, and He fulfills that promise through His Holy Eucharist. Think about it. Through the Eucharist, Jesus can literally and physically be in all places at once.

Spending time in prayer with and before the Blessed Sacrament (the Eucharist) is a form of prayer known as Adoration. It has been a popular devotion in our Church for centuries. Modern day saints like Blessed Mother Teresa of Calcutta and St. John Paul II spent at least an hour a day (if not several) before Jesus in the Blessed Sacrament.

Adoration is not to be confused with Communion. During Communion at Mass, we consume the Lord along with the rest of the community of believers. Think of Adoration as a different kind of prayer time, some one-on-one time to just sit in the presence of the Lord and let Him consume you with His attention and love.

Sometimes there is the temptation to bring "holy things to do" into Adoration because we struggle with just sitting still and praying. It's not that you shouldn't read Scripture or holy books during Adoration, only that sometimes having nothing to read or do forces you to be more present to His presence which is the greatest present you could present. You wouldn't go over to your friend's house, sit across the table from them, and then proceed to read a book *about* them (rather than conversing with your friend) would you?

St. John Vianney once said, "When Our Lord sees pure souls coming eagerly to visit Him in the Blessed Sacrament He smiles on them." He had a strong devotion to the Eucharist and encouraged frequent visits to the Blessed Sacrament for Adoration. One famous story involved a parishioner who would tell St. John Vianney of his time sitting before the Blessed Sacrament in silence who told the saint, "I look at Him, and He looks at me" (*CCC* 2715).

It's that simple, really. You don't have to say a thing if you don't want to. Don't wait for the next Life Teen camp, retreat, or conference to experience Adoration. No, stop by the chapel anytime and give the Lord 15 minutes or an hour. Your soul will soon long for more time there. Wait and see.

REFERENCES

Luke 1:46-49, 10:38-42, 18:1, Deuteronomy 6:13, Sirach 50:17, Isaiah 49:7

CCC 2096-97, 2626-28, 2715, 1378-1379

For more about adoration, including the prayers, insights, and guidance on "how to" focus during this form of prayer, check out "Come Adore" in Life Teen's online store.

73. SILENCE

From the first annoying sounds of the alarm in the morning to the final phrases uttered on the television, tablet, or phone before bed, the day can become an incessant flurry of audio and visual waves buzzing around us. If it's not the music, then it's the shows or movies; if it's not people talking, it is the sound of technology and advertising surrounding us. If you're like me, you probably don't take as much silent time as you should or could (i.e. time with no technology, no television, and no music around you). Finding silence is difficult these days.

Some days it is almost impossible. Or is it?

Silence is not so much a treasure to be found, but a necessity to be cherished. Silence sometimes eludes you and me because we are unwilling to let it find us in our overly busy schedules. The truth is not only that we *need* silence in our days, weeks and lives, but that silence is one of the best and most frequent communication channels that God uses.

There is a famous episode in the Scriptures in which God speaks to the prophet Elijah. You may have heard of it or read it before. Quiet yourself now and read **1 Kings 19:11-13** as if it were your first time.

Yes, God speaks to us in bold ways. God also speaks to us in whispers. What is God saying to you this day? Can you even hear Him or is it difficult? Are there too many voices competing for your attention, too many things vying for your affection? Spend some time in silence. God gave you two ears and one mouth. Use them proportionally. Listen twice as much as you speak. That rule applies in prayer, as well.

Do yourself a favor this week. Turn off your radio when you're in the car, and just allow God to speak to you in the silence. When you're at home tonight, go to bed earlier than normal. Before you fall asleep, instead of talking to God, listen to Him. Sometime this week get to a church on your own when it's empty. Take 15 or 20 minutes and sit in silence in the house of God. Let Him do the talking for a change...

REFERENCES

1 Kings 19:9-13, Esther 10, Isaiah 29:4, Deuteronomy 27:9, Psalm 62:1-5, Habakuk 2:20

CCC 2628, 2717

74. FIGHTING DISTRACTIONS DURING PRAYER

Distraction is a part of life. We can't control the things that happen around us anymore than we can control all the things that happen to us. However, there are ways to take ourselves out of the path of distraction and place ourselves in the path of grace (of God). That does not mean that all distractions will be eliminated. The devil wants to distract you and will use any means possible to do so (1 Peter 5:8), to keep you from God. However, there are things you can do to better direct and focus yourself in your prayer life and spiritual life, as a whole.

Here's a brief list of suggestions:

1. Create a prayerful environment.
We can often get distracted because we are in distracting places. Quiet time is essential, especially in the early stages, for maturing in your prayer life. If you can't learn to pray in silence, you won't learn in the midst of noise. Go into your room and close the door. Possibly play some quiet music. Turn off your phone. Light a candle (but don't fall asleep... a four-alarm fire is not a relaxing prayer environment).

Better yet, get to the chapel at your church and sit as close to the tabernacle as possible. Don't forget your posture. Kneeling goes a long way in helping us to focus ourselves. It's important to be comfortable, but if you're too comfortable you might fall asleep. Vary your posture to ensure your awareness.

2. Offer up distractions for God's glory.

If you find your mind constantly wandering while you pray, offer up those distractions to God. I mean that literally. Say to God, "Lord, you know how consumed I am with this relationship or this situation right now, I offer them up for your glory." If the distractions are being placed there by the devil (to keep you from prayer), the distractions will vanish; the devil will never do anything that gives glory to God. If they are not from the devil then take that as a sign that God wants you to pray about that relationship or situation. Talk to Him about it and ask yourself the tough question... not "What do I want?" but "What does God want?" and "What is God's will?"

3. Utilize guided prayers and meditations.

The Church is such a great guide for us. She gives us prayers for every moment and occasion. You always have the Our Father as the ultimate prayer. In addition, you have the Hail Mary, which, if prayerfully recited, will take you to deep levels of meditation, unlock amazing insight and bring great grace. There are thousands of guided meditations, novenas, and prayers of consecration. You could spend hours online or in bookstores sorting through an endless treasure trove of incredible, prayerful insights that will lead you deeper into the very heart of God. Guided prayers can focus your prayer even when your mind is racing and you might find it difficult to concentrate. Take advantage of the richness and beauty of our 2,000-year tradition as Church.

4. Become an intercessor.

How many of your prayers incorporate "I" or "me"? That doesn't make you bad, it makes you (and I) human. It's not to say you can't or shouldn't ever pray for yourself. Proportionally, how often do you pray for yourself and how often for others? Spend more time as an intercessor. Let your prayers be intercessions for others. The power of prayer is unmistakable. If you doubt your own prayer power, think again. You can't change people, but never underestimate the power, by God's grace, for others to change.

Happy praying!

REFERENCES

Matthew 6:6, Romans 15:30, Colossians 4:3, Ephesians 6:18-19, Hebrews 12:1, Luke 10:40

CCC 2734, 2634-263

For more in-depth guidance and explanation of prayer and its different forms, check out "Come Pray" from the online store at www.lifeteen.com.

MORALITY

75. HUMAN DIGNITY

Human beings have a special place in creation — God made us in His image and became one of us. As such, each human life is sacred and important.

The most basic, fundamental foundation for our treatment of other people can be found in Genesis. Each human being is created in the "image and likeness" of God (Genesis 1:26-27). That doesn't mean that we need to pray to each other; it means that we need to treat each person as we would treat Jesus.

God did not make us objects to be used by each other. Therefore, anytime we treat another human being as an object, we are objectifying Christ. We are all part of the Body of Christ; each one of us is like a cell with a role to play. We should not treat another part of the Body of Christ as an object, no matter how small or insignificant it is in our eyes. That is like treating someone as something that he or she is not. Everyone is human, a child of God and part of the Body, and should be treated as such.

How many times do you not give someone the benefit of the doubt when you should? How many times do you assume that someone is out to get you? How many times do you hold a grudge, finding it hard to forgive? How many times have you treated someone as an object, simply a tool for you to use for your own selfish desires?

These are all crimes against the dignity of the human person. All of us, by virtue of being the image and likeness of God, have an imprint on our soul, the ghost of God in each of us. We are each a part of the body of Christ and we need to treat each human being as such.

There are a lot of people today that feel that we need to instill self-respect and pride in our youth. The truth is we need to impress upon all human beings that each soul and body is a deliberate creation of God and we need to do everything we can to love those around us. That means that we need to sacrifice for the good of the other person. That is how we share our dignity as creations of God.

Life begins in the womb and ends in the tomb. The dignity of both womb and tomb were raised by the virtue of Christ's presence in both. We cannot be partially behind the Gospel of life; we must embrace all of it, for all life comes from God.

"As you did it to one of the least of these my brethren, you did it to me." (Matthew 25:40)

REFERENCES

Psalm 139:14-16, 127:3-5, Genesis 1:26-27, Isaiah 41:10, 44:2, 49:16, Matthew 10:30, Job 10:8-12, Ecclesiastes 11:5, Jeremiah 1:5

CCC 27, 357, 1700, 1703, 2258, 2319, 2393

76. SOCIAL JUSTICE

Christ had a special affection for the poor and the outcast — so much so that it caused controversy with the upper class of the time. If we are to be imitators of Christ we need to imitate his special love and affection.

It is easy to fall into the trap of making money our god. Social justice is a way we can be more like Christ, through a Catholic perspective on the economy and the world we live in. We view money as a tool to help those who need it. There are people that have been placed in our lives so that we may see them and imitate Christ; it gives us a chance to be Christ.

We become Christ when we give from our need, not from our want. When we advocate for those who cannot speak for themselves. We become Christ when we enter into relationship with those who have no one to speak for them. The most forceful voice of this "preferential option for the poor" is Pope Francis. He has, since the beginning of his leadership, shown that he is willing to enter into relationship with the poor.

Building showers and barbershops for the homeless in Rome.

Visiting the poorest neighborhoods in Rio during World Youth Day.

Expressing his desire that the Catholic Church be a poor Church united with the poor.

It isn't that this perspective has been missing or that it is unique, it is simply that it is the main "flavor" or focus of this particular Bishop of Rome. When the disparity between the rich and the poor grows ever wider in our world, it is a focus that is truly needed.

While there are many great things about capitalism, we must understand that profit cannot be the only reason for pursuing our economic goals. It was once said that Christ isn't against the rich, but we will be asked two questions when we accumulate wealth: how did we get the money, and what do we do with it when we have it?

If we profit from treating human beings as objects, then we have made money into something bigger than God. The economy exists to serve people; people do not exist to serve the economy. With wealth comes the moral responsibility to recognize that those who need our help — "To whom more is given, more is expected." This includes countries blessed with economic wealth.

When we use our economic blessings to help those in need, we become Christ for the poor and help Christ at the same time, allowing others to become what Christ intends them to be in the Body. Never forget that being a Catholic Christian means being Christ, even when it hurts.

REFERENCES

Matthew 5:3-12, 25: 31-46, Luke 22:27, 2 Maccabees 9:15, 2 Corinthians 8:13-14, Philippians 2:6

CCC 1928-1942

77. STEM CELL RESEARCH AND RESPONSIBLE SCIENCE

God created humanity with intellect and reason and the free will to use both to glorify God and help our neighbor. For this reason, the Catholic Church has been a champion in the scientific field since it's very beginnings. It is strange, then, that recently many have tried to argue that the Church is "anti-science" or against reason. This could not be further from the truth. The Church does, however, teach that there are appropriate moral boundaries to scientific endeavors, even if the outcome of those projects seems good.

Recently, a major area of misunderstanding of Catholic teaching regarding appropriate moral boundaries for science revolved around stem cell research. It is important to understand the Church's teaching on this topic, and to also view the Church's teaching on ethics in science more broadly.

Stem cell research can be beneficial. It offers an ability and promise to treat many diseases that afflict people today. Already, stem cells are used to treat more than seventy different diseases. The controversy lies in how the stem cells are harvested for research.

There are two ways of getting stem cells. One method has been around for merely forty years, and has paved the way for the treatments that we currently have today. This method uses stem cells gathered form the marrow inside adult bones through a process that does not cause loss of life. This gives us the benefit of science without any morally evil act.

When we obtain stem cells in a way that kills human beings, we defeat the purpose of the research in the first place. Some stem cells are gathered when human life at its beginning stages, stripping the stem cells from human embryos. This kills the person who was growing. Killing people and using their body parts for others is a step backward for humanity and it sounds like a bad story from the Holocaust.

As Catholics, we have a duty to use science for the benefit of humanity by increasing our knowledge of the way that the world works and helping those who can use it. We must never use science to exploit those who need our protection the most.

REFERENCES

Psalm 139:14-16, Genesis 1:26-27, Jeremiah 1:5, Matthew 10:30, Isaiah 44:2, 49:16, Psalm 127:3-5, Job 10:8-12, Ecclesiastes 11:5

CCC 2292, 2295, 1703

78. EUTHANASIA

The only thing that makes a story worth telling is the underlying and fundamental certainty that life is worth living.

Think of any great story. Every one of them is built upon this premise. If they weren't, there is no real conflict; instead of fighting courageously when one encounters overwhelming odds or faces an impossible situation, the characters would simply die. The reasonable thing would be to take matters into one's own hands and end one's life. If they're going to die eventually, why not simply face death on one's own terms?

Because life is worth living.

There is a real difference between a human being and any other kind of animal. Because we are human, we don't merely experience pain... we can also "suffer." Suffering is only possible when you are aware that you are suffering. People are aware when they are suffering; animals do not have the same self-awareness. A human being can look up from their battle and ask "Why?" An animal doesn't ask this question. This makes human suffering exponentially worse than animal suffering... but also exponentially more meaningful.

There is something in us that recognizes that human suffering, while not pleasant, is worth it. We intrinsically know that life is worth living. When we see someone endure suffering heroically, even if it costs them everything, we see human dignity in action. It is the reason why we cheer for those who are willing to face unstoppable odds. It is the reason we love heroes...they remind us that life is worth fighting for. They remind us that there is more to this life.

As Christians, we know that suffering is not the worst thing. Yes, if all there is in this universe is the material world (no soul, no spirit, no God), then the worst possible evil is suffering. But we know that there is more to this life than what we can immediately see.
Dignity is not found in taking one's own life, but in facing the challenge well. Compassion is not helping another person to end their own life, but in caring for them in their weakness and pain.

Jesus has given human suffering a power and a purpose. Jesus reveals that all life, even the most painful and broken life, has the ability to make a difference in this world. When Blessed Chiara had given away every thing that she had and was unable to hardly speak, much less move, she stated, "I have nothing left, but I still have my heart, and with that I can always love."

We have truly lost our way if we equate the term "care" with "assisted suicide." For as long as medicine has existed, there have been strict rules for those charged with the responsibility to care for the suffering, the first of those rules is: "Do no harm." How have we lost this first of commissions?

We have forgotten what it is to be a human being.

Our culture has exchanged a "Sanctity of Life" ethic for a "Quality of Life" ethic. In doing so, we have positioned ourselves to rate a person's worth based off of our perceived quality of their life. We think, "I wouldn't want to have to live like that" and in our fear, we forget the truth: life is worth living.

This is where a heroic life could be made. "Death with dignity" does not mean dying like an animal; it means dying like a human being, with untold worth and courage. Not taking one's own life, but living it out until the end of the story.

REFERENCES

Exodus 20:13, John 10:10, 16:33, 1 Corinthians 3:16-17, 6:19-20, Psalm 23:4, 34:19, 116:15, Romans 8:32-37, 2 Corinthians 12:9, Revelation 21:3-4, James 4:7, Ecclesiastes 3:1-2

CCC 2324, 2276-79

This section is adapted from Fr. Mike Schmitz's article "Courage for the Fight: A Life Worth Living" found on the Life Teen blog at www.lifeteen.com.

79. STANDING UP FOR YOUR FAITH

If you live the way you are supposed to live, you will be persecuted.

Do you agree with that statement above? It's true. Living as a Christian, especially as a Catholic, means you're going to get persecuted by people, Christians and non-Christians (unfortunately even other Catholics) sometimes.

Jesus didn't promise that following Him would be easy. Although He promised to always be with us (Matthew 28:20), and that we'd be more powerful with the Holy Spirit (John 16:7). He promised, in fact, just the opposite. Read Luke 9:23, 12:51 and John 15:18, 16:33.

In every moment of every day, you have a choice to live for God or for the world, to choose Jesus or to choose self. Choosing God takes courage. Choosing God takes faith. Choosing God takes surrendering to Him.

"This last step in the quest for surrender can be the most difficult one. It was for me. I had reached the point where I could admit my sinfulness and knew that I had to change my attitude. But total abandonment to the Holy Spirit was the real leap. What are you prepared to do for God? Are you willing to be uncomfortable or lonely? Are you willing to forego financial security? Are you willing to move, to change or to start over at this stage in your life? If not, admit it. If so, you're ready to abandon yourself to God.

At this point, some people run in the opposite direction. Others stop and some courageously battle forward. I've seen the look in the eyes and the resolve in the legs of those who do continue ahead. They walk through the mockery of classmates and co-workers. They dance while others sit. They drink from the cup of life that God reserves for those who trust Him. They might not have the most money, but they do have the most power.

In the end, it's going to be between you and God. If you fear what he might say, change. If you don't, stay humble and faithful. If you're not sure, think harder."[5]

Don't worry about the words you'll say when others want to question you or debate with you (Luke 21:14-15). The Holy Spirit will speak for you.

Read and pray 2 Timothy 1:7. Commit that verse to memory. God is going to use you. Others aren't always going to like it. Walk in love and live in humility. God will do great things in you.

REFERENCES

1 Timothy 1:19, Matthew 5:11, 44, 10:19, 24:9, Romans 12:14, 2 Corinthians 12:10

CCC 162, 2088

80. THE TEN COMMANDMENTS

Upon first glance it might seem like the Ten Commandments are little more than a list of rules to keep you out of hell. If you've ever thought that way, know that you are not the first to make that mistake. Since the Commandments come from Scripture (Exodus 20), let's use Scripture to take another look and get a better understanding of the kind of life God is calling you to live daily.

It helps to realize Jesus came not to abolish the law, but to complete it (Matthew 5:17). He came to show us how to "have life and have it abundantly" (John 10:10).

Let's take a look at the 10 Commandments in a new way, seen not only as a list of "thou shalt not's," but as a list that fulfills God's law, a list of "thou shalt's":

The Law (Commandments)
Thou shalt not...

...have other gods before me.
...take the Lord's name in vain.
...dishonor the Sabbath.
...dishonor thy father and mother.
...kill.
...commit adultery.
...steal.

...bear false witness.
...covet thy neighbor's wife (lust).
...covet thy neighbor's material goods.

The Life in Christ (fulfillment)
Thou shalt...

...be single-hearted toward me.
...be reverent in speech and conduct.
...keep priorities.
...be respectful and obedient.
...defend life: womb to tomb.
...be faithful to vocation and/or future spouse.
...be trustworthy.
...be honest in word and deed.
...have only pure admiration.
...be grateful for what you possess.

Do you get it? Living a faith-filled life is not so much about what we shouldn't do as about what we are called to do as we move forward in God's love. You can use this parallel above as the beginning of your examination of conscience the next time you prepare for the Sacrament of Reconciliation. In particular, ask yourself how you measure up to the second list (The Life in Christ) as you ready your soul for the sacramental mercy of Christ.[6]

The Ten Commandments aren't just rules. That would mean we were living for a "what" rather than a "who." When we sin, it's not about breaking the Heavenly Judge's rules, it's about breaking our Heavenly Father's heart.

REFERENCES

Exodus 20, 34:28, Deuteronomy 4:13, 10:4, Matthew 5:17

CCC 2058, 2067

81. THE BEATITUDES: THE WORK OF THE CHURCH

Every Catholic should know the Beatitudes. Taken from the Sermon on the Mount they are the most well known – but least well-lived – way of life. Jesus offers them to mankind to show the attitudes we need in order to be part of the Heavenly Kingdom.

Blessed are the poor in spirit for theirs is the Kingdom of Heaven. The "poor in spirit" refers to those who are humble, without pride. There is only one God and He isn't us! Notice that, when we are poor in spirit, we *will* have the Kingdom of Heaven. It isn't something that we will have to wait for.

Blessed are those who mourn for they shall be comforted. Usually, we mourn because we have loved someone. It isn't often that you see someone in pain because he or she has lost someone he or she didn't like. The more we love, the more we suffer, because love involves sacrifice. Christ offers comfort to those who love much.

Blessed are the meek, for they shall inherit the earth. Since the meek know God is in charge, they are willing to accept authority in their own lives as a reflection of the Heavenly authority of God. This acceptance of authority in our lives reduces our dependency on our own pride. As St. John the Baptist said, "He must increase and I must decrease." This humility, this meekness, is a key to inheriting eternal life.

Blessed are those who hunger and thirst for righteousness, for they shall be filled. Righteousness is everything it its right order. Noah loved righteousness. Throughout the Old Testament we have stories of righteous men and women. Do we yearn for everything to be in its right order with God at the top, the way we hunger and thirst for food and water?

Blessed are the merciful, for they shall receive mercy. If you combine this with the Our Father's command to "forgive us as we forgive those who trespass against us," there is a very clear directive. If we do not forgive people in our lives, we will not be forgiven. Mercy is costly; mercy hurts. But Christianity is not about counting the cost.

Blessed are the pure of heart, for they shall see God. Are we pure of heart? Do we desire God above all things, or are we infatuated with earthly pleasures like sex? It is different to be obsessed with God and tempted by sex than to be obsessed with sex but tempted by God.

Blessed are the peacemakers, for they will be called sons of God. Those who strive for peace in all situations and look for peace above all will simply be called "sons of God." If we are working for peace and striving for it in our lives, we are already the sons and daughters of God. It is when others in the world recognize it that the actual title will be given to us.

Blessed are those who are persecuted for righteousness' sake, for theirs is the Kingdom of Heaven. When we are persecuted, things are taken away from us. If we are persecuted because we seek righteousness, the things that are taken away don't mean as much because we understand the correct order of things. When we understand the correct order of things, we recognize what the Lord wants of us.

REFERENCES

Leviticus 19:18, Matthew 5:43, 19:19, 22:39, Romans 13:9, Galatians 5:14, James 2:8

CCC 1716-1728

82. JUST WAR DOCTRINE

The idea of a war seems completely against what Christ came to teach. We often make the mistake of thinking there are two different Gods at work in the Bible: the God of the Old Testament and the God of the New Testament. As if God had a Son and suddenly mellowed out from all of the "smiting" He did for the first 9,000 years of Biblical history.

There is one God. When it comes to the Old and New Testament, it is the same God. The same God whose love heals and brings peace is the same God whose love brings torment to the evil ones, whose justice is seen as cruelty.

We live in an imperfect world and as human beings we continually fall in our journey home to heaven. When you gather a large group of people together into a country or region, the mistakes can take global proportions. Often these imperfections, misunderstandings and even evil can result in war.

Under what grounds would it be moral for a Catholic to engage in war?

Over the last 2,000 years, the "Just War" theory has outlined the parameters for a Roman Catholic to engage in any war (*CCC* 2309):

1. The war must involve a real, lasting, grave or serious, and certain damage that would be inflicted by the aggressor.

2. War must be the last resort, with all other options exhausted.

3. The rights and values at stake in the conflict justify killing to defend them.

4. There can be no needless destruction, cruelty to prisoners, or harsh measures such as torture.

5. Only the proper representatives of the people have a right to declare a war of defense.

6. A chance of success must exist to prevent a hopeless use of force.

7. War must never create worse evils than the evil being eliminated.

REFERENCES

John 14:27, 20:19-21, Luke 19:42, Ephesians 2:14, Galatians 5:22, Leviticus 26:6, Numbers 13, Judges 3:10, 5:8, 10:17-18

CCC 2309

83. THE CHURCH'S TEACHING ON HOMOSEXUALITY

There are many common misinterpretations of the Church's stance on homosexuality and they usually sound something like, "The Church hates homosexuals," or "You can't be homosexual and Catholic." Neither of these are true.

The Catholic Church recognizes that sexual relationships are very powerful — so powerful that they can create a human life. It has an incredible power to connect a couple, cementing their spiritual bond and relationship. This is why the sexual act should be reserved solely for marriage. Only in marriage can a couple experience the benefits of sexuality mentioned above. If you are going to bond with someone or have children with that person, you should be joined with him or her for life in vows made before God, family, and friends.

It is important to understand that those who struggle with homosexual desires do not sin unless they entertain those desires in lust. The same standards apply to heterosexual desires. There is no special asterisk next to homosexuality as though it is a special sin just because someone is tempted. God will always honor those who turn to Him in times of temptation.

Why will the Church not marry homosexual couples – especially as it seems that more states and countries are allow "gay marriage"? For the simple reason that it is outside of the plan of God for marriage, through which children can be conceived. Marriage reflects God in a special way through the creative aspect of marriage. Humans procreate through the sexual act, which (also given by God), serves two purposes: to be unifying and procreative. When we remove one of those elements the act loses its intended purpose.

Marriage reflects the love that God has within the Trinity, a love that ultimately becomes a creative force. A requirement of marriage is that it is entered into willingly, faithfully, and that a couple promises to be open to the gift of children from God. These are not arbitrary decisions some person made thousands of years ago, but divine truths that were given to us by God.

Therefore, marriage should not be extended to those who would like to marry children, animals, or those who wish to engage in polygamy. The reason is because we recognize that marriage is sacred, special, and holy. If we become the authors of marriage instead of God and change the standards He has set, we will quickly find ourselves changing the rules whenever our moods change.

The Church does not "doom" a person that experiences same-sex attraction to a life of loneliness. God does not call everyone to marriage, and many homosexual persons live the Church's teaching faithfully with the help of friends and family. There are many ways to experience relationships, marriage is one of them but it is not the only one. Every person is called to experience love uniquely and within God's plan.

It is important to pray for those who struggle with sexual temptation, especially homosexuality. We must never discriminate against them or treat them differently because of the struggles they may have — our own struggles are difficult enough to deal with, and we would never want to be treated differently because of them. Jesus would simply love us, and encourage us to always find comfort in Him.

REFERENCES

Genesis 1:26-28, 19:13, Romans 1:26-28, 1 Corinthians 6:9, 10:13, 1 Timothy 1:9-10, Leviticus 18:22, 20:13, Ezekiel 16:50

CCC 2357-2359

84. ABORTION

Biologically, life begins at conception. There is only one moment during which we can be sure there is something there that did not exist before and that is when the sperm and the egg join together to form a zygote, or the very first stage of human life. At that point, a person has all of the DNA he or she will ever need. If left in an environment that is safe, which is the uterus of the mother, that person may grow and lead a healthy life. Abortion deliberately stops the growth of that human and removes its ability to live. It kills the human being.

There is no other way to put it. Before an abortion, a woman is pregnant. After an abortion, a woman is not pregnant. Before an abortion, there is a life that needs to be nourished, supported, and cared for. After an abortion, that life is no longer there.

In a world where it is common for human beings to be treated as objects, we can often go through our lives without thinking about the tragedy that is abortion, a tragedy that kills thousands every day simply because the human being is "inconvenient" and doesn't fit into another human's plans.

God has a plan and His plan involves each of us. In order to fulfill His plan, each of us needs to be allowed to fulfill our potential. When we prevent others from doing so it is a grave crime. Even if the beginning of a person's life involved pain from rape or incest, crimes that cry out to God due to their tragic nature, that new life is not to blame.

No one can tell the future. But know the plans He has for us are good, and not harmful. Perhaps you find yourself in a situation where you don't think you can care for a child, or don't think the child will live the kind of life you want him or her to. Part of being Catholic is recognizing that things don't always happen according to our plans. *God's plan is much bigger than us*. When we try to force our plans on the world, we damage the plans of God.

The damage does not end there. If you have been damaged by abortion, know that you are in our prayers. Also know that there needs to be a healing. There are resources for those who have gone through an abortion or been a part of one. It is important that you take advantage of those resources.

REFERENCES

Matthew 10:30, 18:10, Exodus 21:22-23, Luke 1:15, Genesis 1:26-27, 9:6, Psalm 127:3-5, 139:14-16, Jeremiah 1:5, Isaiah 44:2, 49:16, Job 10:8-12, Ecclesiastes 11:5

CCC 2271-2274, 2770

85. FORGIVENESS

What do forgiveness and nuclear physics have in common? That's right... neither are easy.

Most of you have probably heard the quote, "To err is human, to forgive divine." That's pretty cool. Have you ever *really* thought about that quote? I'll be honest; forgiveness has not always been easy for me. There are people who have really hurt me in the past. I mean really hurt me. You can relate, right? It isn't always easy to truly forgive. In fact, it's almost never easy.

Yet in the Our Father we give God permission to forgive us to the same extent that we forgive others who've hurt us. Speaking personally, that's pretty scary when I think about it.

So often, forgiveness is like the last piece of gum: Everyone wants it, but no one wants to give it up. Let's get practical for a minute. If you found out that you were going to die in 15 minutes, and you only had time to call one or two people (besides your family), who would it be? Would it be someone you needed to forgive or someone you needed to ask forgiveness from? Next question: What are you waiting for?

Make the call, write a letter, send an email — life is too short.

"If you forgive others their transgressions, your heavenly Father will forgive you. But if you do not forgive others, neither will your Father forgive your transgressions." (Matthew 6:14-15)

Let the weak hold their grudges; it takes a much stronger person to forgive.

Spend some time in prayer on this topic. Grab your Bible for some guidance.

Good verses about the need to forgive others

Matthew 6:12, 14-15
Matthew 18:21-35
Luke 6:37, 17:3-4
1 Corinthians 13:5
Ephesians 4:32
Colossians 3:12-13
2 Corinthians 2:7

Good verses about how God forgives

Matthew 6:14-15
Psalm 32:5, 86:4-7, 103:12
Proverbs 28:13
Daniel 9:9
Isaiah 55:6,7
Jeremiah 33:8
Matthew 11:28-30
Luke 1:77
Romans 8:1
Ephesians 1:7-8

Hebrews 8:12
James 5:15-16
1 John 1:9

REFERENCES

CCC 2840, 2845

86. CHASTITY

Have you ever felt that "tug-o-war" in your soul, when your body wants to go in one direction but your soul is calling you in another? That voice calling you to holiness is the Holy Spirit. Do you know that feeling, like your body and soul are locked in an epic battle between what feels good and what you know is right?

You're not alone. Everyone, both saints and sinners, know the battle well. What separates the saints from sinners is their response to the battle and who they let win it.

A lot of people think that chastity is "not having sex." That's not it — that definition doesn't come close to explaining the beautiful truth of chastity. Chastity is not merely abstinence; it is more than whether or not you have sex.

Check out how the Catechism defines and describes chastity: "Chastity means the successful integration of sexuality within the person and thus the inner unity of man in his bodily and spiritual being" (*CCC* 2337).

Chastity is not just about getting the body and soul, the flesh and spirit, working in rhythm and out of that "tug-o-war," it's about directing both toward God (love). "Chastity is the virtue that directs our sexual desires and attitudes toward the truth of love."[7] That is why sexual intercourse is reserved for the Sacrament of Marriage. Marriage is designed to be the living, physical embodiment of sacrificial (not selfish) love. That's right, married people live chastity too.

Yes, "...you were created with desires (but that) does not mean that those desires should dictate your life, your relationships, environments, social life, or dress. Sex, in and of itself, should not become the motivating factor or the goal of life that many allow it to become. Sex is not power. Sex is not a mere act. Sex is a language, gifted to us by God that speaks of commitment and self-sacrifice. Sex is an expression of unconditional love, a unifying experience for two people who have offered their lives to one another, before God and witnesses."[8]

Chastity is living properly and happily. Living chastity means you will no longer be consumed with guilt or shame. Living chastity helps you to grasp the bigger purpose of your life and of your body. It teaches us the difference, sexually, between purpose and use. If you have never read or heard about the *Theology of the Body*, you owe it to yourself to learn about it. It is one of the greatest gifts St. John Paul II gave us during his pontificate. It is a gift to the 21st century. Get a copy, it will change the way you view not only chastity, but your body, your life, and your vocation.

REFERENCES

1 Peter 3:2-7, 2 Timothy 2:22, 2 Peter 2: 9-10, Matthew 15:18-19, James 1:14-15, 1 Corinthians 6:12-20

CCC 2337, 2348, 2394

Jason Evert's chastity resources are a great place to start if you are desiring a more expansive explanation of the Church's teachings regarding chastity – check out www.chastityproject.com.

87. JUDGING OTHERS

When I began getting into my faith, I could not figure out why it had to be so difficult. The minute you start to try to love like Jesus or live in His image, you get attacked. St. Paul warned us about that (Romans 7:21). What surprised me though was how I was attacked and who it was that I struggled with.

I expected those who were opposed to Christ and who didn't like His Gospel to attack me. I anticipated long debates with people who had been turned off by religion, who felt let down by God, or who felt that faith wasn't logical. I expected those hurdles. No problem, it just took time and growing in patience, humility, and wisdom on my part.

As a teenager, I didn't expect so many "Christians," Catholics as well as non-Catholics, to make my life far more difficult than any atheist. I never expected my brothers and sisters in the faith to be so hurtful, so judgmental, and at times, so merciless. I wasn't prepared for the people I prayed with on Sundays to be so hypocritical on Fridays. I didn't know how to handle everything I was seeing. That was until I looked in the mirror. Then my world really came apart.

The truth was that I had absolutely no right to condemn, judge, or get frustrated with others trying to live their faith, until I made changes to my own faith. Judgment is a tricky word. We're told not to judge by

Jesus (Matthew 7), and that is correct. We should not judge others' hearts when our hearts are filled with sin. We're also told by Jesus though that "if a brother sins, rebuke him; if he repents, forgive him" (Luke 17:3), reminding us that we should call each other out of our sin.

It is possible to judge the sin and the action as contrary to Jesus, without judging the person or the heart. When a believer, a true Christian does call someone out however, they should be someone who is making a conscious and deliberate effort to follow God on their own; otherwise they will be seen as just another hypocrite. Jesus was not a "do as I say, not as I do" Son, He was a "do as I do, love as I love" Savior.

To quote Sirach 2:15, "Those who love Him, keep His ways." What a great reminder for me before I call someone out. I know if I am keeping His ways. You know if you are too. If you are, keep it up. If you're not, how come?

No one said that Christianity would be easy once you got to know Him. On the contrary, it's once you get to know Him that it gets harder, but also more fulfilling. He loves you. Love Him back.

Who knows, the life you change for Christ today, might just be your own.

REFERENCES

Matthew 6:14-15, 7:1-5, Romans 2:1-2, 1 Corinthians 4:5

CCC 679, 1777-82, 681, 2477-78, 1861-2497

88. THE DEATH PENALTY

One of the most hotly debated issues among practicing Catholics is that of the death penalty. Many struggle with the fact that the Church speaks out against it, even in the case of hardened criminals who have admitted they are guilty of the crimes for which they were convicted. People often quote Scripture passages like "an eye for an eye" (Matthew 5:38) in hopes of justifying their personal feelings that oppose Church teachings.

Essentially, the idea of the death penalty has been the protection of society against people that would cause further damage to the public. In the last fifty years, it has become increasingly easy for government officials to protect a society from even the most dangerous criminals through advancements in the modern methods of imprisonment.

There is a part of us as human beings, a natural inclination, that desires revenge. We would like to see someone pay "the ultimate price" for doing something horrible to others. However, that innate desire for vengeance is actually rooted in sin. It is at this time that we need to forgive: when it is hardest, when someone has hurt us so deep it seems that we are on a cross. Yet, too many times our desire for revenge clouds our judgment.

Every person should be given the best possible chance at heaven. If that means that we need to keep them in prison for life, then that is what we need to do. When we execute someone, we cut short their opportunity to experience a conversion, a change of heart so that they can experience the unconditional love and limitless mercy of God.

Consider that if we are going to be defenders of human life at the beginning by opposing abortion, then it is reasonable for us to defend human life at the end, even if that life is difficult to love and forgive due to the choices made.

When in doubt, we will never go wrong by choosing life. Only in the most serious of circumstances should we ever choose to end another person's life. That decision can never be made due to a desire for revenge. If the death penalty is needed to protect the lives of others, it must be a last resort, the only option available to a society, a culture, and the individuals involved.

REFERENCES

John 8:7, Leviticus 19:18, Romans 12:19, Matthew 5:7, 18:33, Psalm 51:1, 119:156, Isaiah 55:7

CCC 2266-67

89. CONTRACEPTION

Contraception is the deliberate manipulation of the sexual act in order to avoid conception. Since sexual relations are to be kept to marriage, it makes sense that one should not use contraception, since one of the purposes of marriage and the sexual relationship is to have children.

In marriage, a couple is responsible for discerning whether they should have children by being accountable to God, each other, the rest of the family and society as a whole. If there is a serious reason to postpone a pregnancy within marriage, a couple should simply abstain from sexual intercourse during the time when the woman is fertile. There is a very scientific method for determining this, called Natural Family Planning, or NFP.

Natural Family Planning is not the "Rhythm Method," nor is it a way for a couple to try to have as many children as possible. The difference between Natural Family Planning and contraception is that Natural Family Planning is always open to life. There is always a possibility that a life could be conceived. In short, the couple is opening itself up to the will of God in their marriage.

When a couple is open to the will of God in their marriage, the burden of when to conceive falls on the both of them rather than one of the two taking a pill or putting a barrier between them.

Spiritually in marriage, two souls join and become one, and the couple also becomes literally one flesh. When they contracept, there is a barrier between the two, both physically and spiritually. The last thing we need is a barrier between spouses or a barrier between God and ourselves. Pray for a greater acceptance of the teaching of God in this area.

REFERENCES

Genesis 1:27-18, Romans 1:25-27, 1 Timothy 2: 11-15, Galatians 6:7, Matthew 21:19 (Mark 11:14), Leviticus 21:17-20

CCC 2370, 2399

90. PORNOGRAPHY

One of the most predominant offenses against the sixth commandment – "thou shalt not commit adultery" – is seen in the form of pornography. Porn is an offense against chastity and a perversion of the sacredness of sex. Porn is a mockery of the intimacy and beauty of Sacramental love. In fact, the very word *pornography* comes from the Greek *pornographos* which means "writing about prostitutes." That's right, pornography is about prostitution. The concept of someone exposing themselves in such a way publicly or surrendering their dignity is linked with prostitution, which is obviously a sin on both peoples' part— the one being viewed and the one viewing.

Pornography destroys a person's capacity to give and receive love properly. It reduces the mystery of sex to mere use, turning something sacred and Godly into something profane and dark. As St. John Paul II said, "The opposite of love is not hate, the opposite of love is use." Pornography is all about self-gratification; pornography is all about use.

Now, I realize that many souls reading this might very likely struggle with pornography or lust, and, quite possibly, masturbation.

Pornography happens when one person uses another for the purpose of indulging his or her lust. This makes the person being used into an object, a tool for the other person to simply use and then discard. That is hardly the way a human being should be treated.

Wherever pornography becomes a part of a society, the habit of using other people increases the occurrences of rape and violent crime. If we treat anther person as a sexual object, it becomes easier to treat others in our lives as different kinds of objects, as well.

Pornography is never something that one usually dreams of being involved in later in life. Usually, if someone is involved in pornography as a business, it is due to a certain amount of desperation, or an attempt at fulfilling a need. In all cases, we must pray for those who are trapped inside this secretive and addictive habit. God wants more from us than to use others, and, if we are caught in this net, we should turn to Mary, the Mother of Purity.

This book and the Commandments, in general, aren't intended to fill souls with shame or guilt. God's truth shines light into darkness; God's truth points you to true freedom.

No sin is bigger than God's grace. If this is a sin that has enslaved you or a temptation that seems too much for you to handle... it's time to reconcile yourself with God. You need the grace of the sacraments, particularly the Sacrament of Reconciliation, to win this battle. God's mercy is bigger than your sin, addiction, or struggle.

REFERENCES

1 Corinthians 6:20, 10:13, Romans 12:1-2, Job 31:1, Ephesians 2:10, 5:8, Jeremiah 1:4-8, James 1:27,

CCC 2211, 2354, 2396

For more information on how to combat pornography, check out "Victory" by Matt Fradd and Mark Hart as well as the companion app found at www.lifeteen.com in the online store.

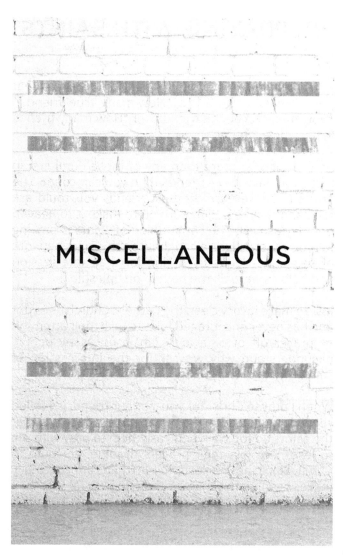

MISCELLANEOUS

91. PRAYING WITH SAINTS

When I ask you, "How many friends do you have?" what pops into your mind? Is it, "How many 'true' friends," "How many Facebook friends," or "How many friends in my whole lifetime"?

Actually, it's far more than any of those numbers. In truth you have more friends than you can count. The saints in heaven are the best friends you could ask for... and they're pulling for you to make it to heaven one day as well. The communion of saints is praying for you constantly. We can draw on this giant network of heavenly friends by asking for their intercession and help as we walk the path of discipleship.

Just to make it very clear, the Catholic Church does not and has never encouraged folks to take their attention or prayer off of or away from Jesus. Many people misunderstand why we ask for the intercession of saints. Think of it this way:

When I pray to Christ for you, as your friend, it's called secondary mediation. I am doing the same thing that the saints do for me when I ask them to pray with me to Jesus... to join their prayers to mine, en route to Christ. Since they're closer to Him than I am, it actually makes even more sense for them to pray for me, than for my earthly friends to pray for me.

The saints in Heaven are alive and are perpetually in prayer. They are absolutely living in Heaven, just as you and I live, but to an even fuller extent, because they are back home with God. He is "the God of the living, not of the dead" (Mark 12:26-27). Since they are far closer to God than we are (2 Corinthians 3:18), as sinful humans walking the earth, their prayers are more powerful.

The saints in heaven are free of all sin, which is what hinders our prayers (Matthew 17:20, 1 John 3:22, Psalms 66:18) and they are in total, perfect union with God.

We are still united with our saintly brothers and sisters (1 Corinthians 12:21-27, Romans 12:5, Ephesians 4:4, Colossians 3:15), as "death cannot separate us from Christ" (Romans 8:35-39).

The saints are praying harder for your salvation than any soul on earth because they know the incredible reality that is heaven. Their hope is that you will join them there at the end of your life and re-unite in one of the most incredible family reunions there has ever been.

REFERENCES

Hebrews 12:1, 18-19, 22-24, Revelation 5:8, 14, Revelation 6:10, 8:3-4

CCC 961-962, 2683

92. HOLY DAYS

As you may or may not know, the word "holiday" is actually a derivation from the Old English phrase, "Holy day." "Holiday" was a shortened way of saying "holy day." These two words are the same; they are intimately linked. Holy days are like holidays for the soul.

The holy days are as follows (*CCC* 2177):

January 1, the solemnity of Mary, Mother of God

Thursday of the Sixth Week of Easter, the solemnity of the Ascension

August 15, the solemnity of the Assumption of the Blessed Virgin Mary

November 1, the solemnity of All Saints

December 8, the solemnity of the Immaculate Conception

December 25, the solemnity of the Nativity of Our Lord Jesus Christ

These are the holy days (and all Sundays) that are generally accepted in the universal Church. In addition to these days, the Catechism also lists the Epiphany and Corpus Christi (both celebrated on a Sunday), the feast of St. Joseph and the feast of Saints Peter and Paul.

And yes, missing Mass on a holy day of obligation is a mortal sin. So don't do it!

Many people look at holy days of obligation as just that, "an obligation." But, we have the gift, the privilege to come together with our brothers and sisters in the presence of God. We get to worship Him in silence and in song, profess our faith, be forgiven for our sins and hear His love letter to us (Scripture). We get to gather around His table and receive the actual, real Body and Blood of our Savior in a form we can take into ourselves, transforming us with His grace and turning us into walking tabernacles. We are strengthened in grace, commissioned and sent forth into a sinful world that desperately needs the Christ we have within us. We are on a mission with Him!

Is that really such a horrific "obligation"?

We should be calling them "Holy Days of opportunity." God is good to us, so good that He offers Mass to us every day. Take advantage of the gift as often as possible, daily if you can. And seriously, don't miss Holy Days, they are great opportunities to grow closer to God.

REFERENCES

Genesis 2:2, Hebrews 12:22-23, Nehemiah 10:31, Isaiah 58:13, Ecclesiastes 3:1

CCC 1389, 2180-2193

93. WHY DO CATHOLICS HAVE THE CRUCIFIX AND NOT "JUST" THE CROSS?

Here's a riddle: "What has to happen before Easter Sunday?"

(If you replied "color eggs" go to the back of the room. Do not pass Go. Do not collect $200).

Before we can get to the glory of the Resurrection (Easter), we have to go through the suffering of the crucifixion (Good Friday). You can't get to the rose without the thorns.

As Catholics we display, wear and process with a crucifix and not "just" a cross. We don't "keep the body on the cross" out of some morbid desire to depress people. The Church has not forgotten the truth and glory of the Resurrection. There is no secret plot at play, no short term memory that wants to somehow "keep Jesus on the cross or in the tomb." No, Catholics raise high the crucifix because we want to proclaim the bigger picture of salvation. Suffering is a beautiful and necessary part of salvation. Life is not just about the shiny golden cross of Easter, that's only half the story. The reality is that life is also about the bloody, splintered cross of Good Friday. Before Christ's crown was gold, it was thorns.

The crucifix ensures that we keep the proper perspective when life is more storms than sunshine. The crucifix is not a symbol of defeat, but of hope.

Suffering is one of the greatest gifts that God can bestow upon His children. It's not a matter of "bad things happening to good people." Quite the contrary, God allows His children to suffer precisely because they are good. Reread the book of Job, not for its literal truth but for its allegorical truths. (Note: allegorical is just a big way of saying that a story that is not necessarily "historically" true can communicate truth, nonetheless.)

God knows well what His children can handle (1 Corinthians 10:13) and allows us to encounter various trials and sufferings so that when others see us endure them and not abandon God, they will seek to know (1 Peter 3:15) where we get such peace in the face of turmoil. That's why St. James tells us to consider it a good thing when we go through hardship (James 1:2-4). It is a sign that God thinks more of you than you do of yourself. What is beautiful in the invitation to take up our crosses and follow Christ is that now, finally, our suffering has purpose. Suffering unites us with Christ.

In the eyes of God, the crucifix is the most glorious sight in the history of humanity. While calling the bloodied and destroyed body of our God "glorious" may seem confusing in the mind of society, it is the most accurate description from God's perspective. The Corpus Christi (body of Christ) that we gaze upon in the crucifix is the highest sign of love this world has ever seen. It is so scandalous and uncomfortable that most would rather view the cross without the corpus.

The love of God is scandalous because it is untamed, unconditional, and unyielding. God the Father did not look down only to see the sin covering His Son, He looked down and saw the selflessness in the sacrifice. When He looked at how abandoned His Son was in the face of suffering, God's heart could not help but be moved by the perfection of love.

REFERENCES

Luke 9:23, Romans 5:3, 8:18, 2 Timothy 2:3, James 1:2, 1 Peter 4:13, Philippians 3:10, Colossians 1:24, 2 Corinthians 1:5

CCC 616-617, 1668-1671, 853, 1182, 1939

94. 666: THE DEVIL'S DIGITS?

Over the centuries, the following verse from Revelation has been one of the most frequently quoted and most often misinterpreted verses within the Scriptures:

"This calls for wisdom: let him who has understanding reckon the number of the beast, for it is a human number, its number is six hundred and sixty-six." (Revelation 13:18)

So, why is the number 666 significant?

You see, while numbers carry symbolic meaning in Scripture, they also carry numeric value, ascribed to letters. In Greek and Hebrew, letters are used for numbers and there is a value (numeric) that corresponds to every letter in those alphabets. In our alphabet, A would be 1 or Z would be 26 – you get the idea. When you add up the values in a name or a word, they will equal a sum total. For instance, say A did equal 1 and N equaled 14: the name "Anna" would equal (1 + 14 + 14 + 1 = 30). Make sense? That being said, the number six hundred-sixty six carries a different meaning and significance depending upon who you choose to listen to on the subject.

Over the years, people have used the number to point to Napoleon Bonaparte, to corrupt Popes, to religious reformers like Martin Luther, to people like

Mussolini, Hitler, and Saddam Hussein. Not long ago, people were doing loose math to ascribe the number to Osama bin Laden. Most Biblical scholars attribute the number to Nero Caesar. If you take the values of the Hebrew consonants in his name they equal 666.

Nero was a vicious Roman emperor and murderer of many Christians in the early Church. It would stand to reason that since Revelation was an apocalyptic book of symbolism and vision given to St. John while he was exiled on the island of Patmos, he would be encouraging the churches under persecution in a time when most of his counterparts and fellow disciples had been martyred for the faith.

Now, as far as the devil is concerned, it's important that you don't mess around with him, for Scripture warns us: "Be sober, be watchful. Your adversary the devil prowls around like a roaring lion, seeking some one to devour (1 Peter 5:8)."

That being said, you need not fear the devil either. The devil is not Jesus' equal, but an angel. The devil is not equal with God. When you are feeling attacked or if you feel the presence of evil, you need only call upon the name of Christ and He will send His angels to surround and protect you. St. Michael kicks the devil's forked tail each and every time. Read **Revelation 12:7-9** for more details, and learn the St. Michael prayer (listed later in this book).

God has the devil's number. God wins the war.

REFERENCES

Matthew 4:1-11, Revelation 12:7-9, 13:18, Romans 7:21, 1 Peter 5:8

CCC 391-398, 2115-2138, 2851-2852, 407-409

95. THINKING ABOUT DRINKING? MAN-MADE LAWS VS. GOD'S NATURAL LAW

Often times as we "get more into our faith," there comes a point where we have to decide whether or not we are really going to submit to God's authority or just continue to play God ourselves. There may be Commandments or laws or rules that we don't agree with and we begin to play word games, bend rules and look for the path of least resistance. Put simply, many Christians then and now sought the Lord but when following Him proved too challenging, began to look, instead, for the loopholes in God's law.

The glorious truth, however, is that there are no "loopholes" in the Bible... we've already looked.

Each conversation is often the same... it is challenging to live a holy life in an unholy culture. Most people are truly looking for the Lord; some, however, are looking less for the Lord and more for the loopholes.

For instance: "I heard that the Bible doesn't say drinking alcohol is a sin."

Well, no, the Bible does not say that drinking alcohol is a sin, but it does become sinful (very easily), if any of the following happen:

- If you are not of legal age. (Romans 13:1-7, Matthew 22:21)

- If you fail to do so in moderation — meaning you should not get drunk or even buzzed. (1 Thessalonians 5:6-8, Galatians 5:21, Romans 12:1-3, 13:13)

- If your consumption leads you to dependence upon it. (1 Timothy 3:8, Titus 2:3, Luke 21:34)

- If doing so *in any way* leads others into sin. (Romans 14:21, 2 Corinthians 6:3, Matthew 13:41)

Some young people embrace these truths and accept them with humility as they try to grow in holiness. Others just try to debate, justify, legitimize, or argue their way around them because they don't like the answer. Here is where the disconnect usually happens. Where do you want your energy to go: toward the Lord or towards some desired loophole?

High school students sometimes argue that they are mature enough to drink alcohol before they're 21. "I can die for my country, but I can't buy a beer," I often hear uttered by seniors.

The question at hand is not your maturity, necessarily. I know plenty of people who are chronologically legal to drink, but far too immature to be doing so. Maturity is about more than age, but *true* maturity also encompasses humility, and wisdom. Obedience is an even greater sign of maturity than courage; it takes courage (and humility) to be obedient.

Some teens say there's just nothing fun to do in their town or argue about how stressful their life is and how they just need a drink to relax. If you *need* alcohol to have fun or to relax, that's a sad statement about your life, your friends, and a probable sign of a far deeper problem like addiction.

Some people just want an excuse... alcohol — to act like an idiot or to be sexually promiscuous without being held too accountable for it. Drunkenness doesn't excuse or justify sins, it adds to the sin and often magnifies them even more. You are not held accountable by God only for what you remember but for what you do.

Others think that drinking alcohol in some way validates and legitimizes them, or makes them more of an adult. This is just stupid. Your worth comes from Jesus Christ, not from drinking. Your dignity comes from God. And while the Bible does not overtly say that drinking alcohol is sinful, it is very, very clear in warning about the dangers and problems that often come with alcohol.

Our holiness is not measured by what *we* want but by what *God* wants for us. Obedience and humility make us holy. An openness to God's grace makes us holy.

Allowing that grace to make us more virtuous makes us holy.

The cup that Christ offers us to drink from is not being passed from a keg... it is a cup of sacrifice, a cup of suffering that comes with putting God's will ahead of our own.

For those of you still reading, I'm proud of you. I'm very proud of you, because your heart is open – maybe more open than you realize – and the Lord wants to speak to that openness.

For those who have gotten angry while reading this — I'd invite you to pray about this more in the Lord's presence. Go before the Blessed Sacrament with your arguments and philosophies and see if the Lord is as supportive of them as your friends are.

God wants us to be pure. God wants us to live for Him. God wants us to be examples. God wants us to lead others to holiness, not to sin. St. Paul called this "the law of love." It basically meant that we should avoid anything that could cause one of our fellow brothers or sisters in Christ to stumble or fall on their walk toward Him.

So where do you want to spend your energy... seeking the Lord or the loopholes?

REFERENCES

Romans 13:13, 1 Corinthians 5:11, 6:9-10, Galatians 5:21, Ephesians 5:18

CCC 2290

96. CATHOLICISM IN THE MEDIA

Quickly name as many movies and television shows as you can in the past 20 years that portray the Catholic Church, her priests and religious, or her faithful followers in a positive light.

How many could you think of? Need more time? Okay take a few more minutes.

How about now?

How many do you have? Not too many are there? That's because, sadly, so few (if any) actually exist. The Catholic Church is painted more negatively and mocked more freely by the media than any other religion or denomination of Christianity. Priests and nuns are painted in broad negative strokes, casting shadows of mistrust and mockery upon their heroic sacrifices. Lay Catholics are normally painted as being mental simpletons who cannot think for themselves and are under the "oppressive mind control" of the evil Church hierarchy. Occasionally, you might see a "likeable" Catholic, but they normally end up being overzealous or "enlightened" (meaning that they "know better" than the Church and hypocritically refuse to live what she teaches).

There are many reasons we could point to for these sad realities. Some Catholics who have left the Church are in need of healing. We need to pray for them and invite them back home. Other people function out of total ignorance of what the Church is really about and what she really teaches. We need to reach out to them in humility and love. Still others are intimidated by the Church's honesty and truth. It calls them to take a difficult look at their own lives. These people need the truth; deep down they even desire it, but not bad enough, not for what it will cost them.

A few years back there was a survey conducted by the Center for Media and Public Affairs in Washington, D.C. It was a survey of the Top 100 media executives in the United States. Basically, these 100 people controlled most of what we read, hear, and see as Americans on a daily basis. These 100 are the "gate keepers," many of whom have the final say in what the general public does and does not see and hear. The following bullet points are facts drawn out of the survey that they answered:

- 93% seldom or never go to religious services

- 97% support abortion

- 80% don't view engaging in homosexual acts as wrong

- 51% don't regard adultery as wrong[9]

The survey alludes to a general trend in some very powerful positions within the entertainment industry. Some of the most fundamental truths that Catholics defend are not only called into question, but are denounced by very influential people.

As a Catholic, you have an opportunity to spread God's truth. The power is yours. What you choose to watch, listen to, and spend your money on is your right. Speak out against people or media that slander your faith. Write letters to people demanding greater respect when you see it compromised.

And never, ever forget how to hit the button marked "off."

REFERENCES

Mark 13:6, Luke 21:8, 2 Timothy 4:1-6, John 16:13, Romans 1:18-32, 7:21, Matthew 7:21

CCC 2496, 2523, 2498

97. THE TRUTH ABOUT OUJI BOARDS, PSYCHICS, MEDIUMS, AND SPIRITUALISM

It's Saturday night and you and your friends have nothing to do. Suddenly, your friend pulls out a Ouija Board. You figure you'll have a laugh and some harmless fun.

But there is a bigger issue at hand. How do you know for sure if what you are dealing with is only harmless fun? In the case of consulting psychics, mediums, or trying to contact the dead, we must be careful. There is only one God and that God has promised to provide for us. When we consult the spiritual world outside of the Church, it is as though we are leaving the protection of the castle. We do not have the authority to deal with opposing forces, and they are free to do with us as they please.

The Church is clear in her teaching against all forms of divination, astrology, trying to communicate with the dead, fortune telling, and other occult-related practices. In both the Old and New Testaments, the people of God are reminded that we can trust God to provide everything we need and that we shouldn't look to other "spirits" or "forces" for special knowledge or powers (Deuteronomy 18:14, Colossians 2:8, *CCC* 2116, 2117, 2138).

The first commandment requires that we have no other gods in our lives; in channeling spirits, we are turning our hearts, our souls, and our worship to other things (and spirits) other than God.

In the case of a medium, especially one on TV, it's very likely that a lot of what we see is just made up. Many self-proclaimed mediums and psychics have been exposed as frauds that just use words that are vague enough that they could apply to anyone.

Another possibility is that the medium or a psychic is actually communicating with an evil spirit (demon) who is posing as a deceased friend or family member. Whenever we try to communicate with other spirits, we open ourselves up to the influence of evil spirits and we invite them into our lives. That's why the Church is so strong in condemning things like Tarot card readings, Ouija boards, fortune-telling, and other attempts to contact (or learn from) spirits other than God.

If we are communicating with something of God, it will always be consistent with the Tradition of the Church, and never teach us to go against what has been revealed by God. If we open ourselves up to communicating with demons, we face powers far beyond our own which we can never hope to control. Remember, Paul warns us that demons can appear even disguised as angels.

If we're concerned about a loved one who died, or if we find ourselves thinking about them a lot, we should always take the opportunity to pray for their soul. We pray that they can be brought from the cleansing purifications of Purgatory to the eternal joy of Heaven. When it comes to knowing things about the future, or even the past, we can trust God. We can trust that He loves us and that He'll reveal to us what we need to know in His perfect time. He's good like that.

REFERENCES

Deuteronomy 18:10, Jeremiah 29:8, Galatians 5:20, Ephesians 5:5, Luke 4:9, 1 Corinthians 10:9

CCC 391-398, 2115-2138, 2851-2852, 407-409

This section is adapted from Brian Kissinger's article "Long Island Medium: Ghosts, God, and the Church" found on the Life Teen blog at www.lifeteen.com

98. ANGELS AND DEMONS AND SPIRITUAL BATTLES

Angels and devils are pure spirit and spirits are all intellect and will. Therefore, angels and devils do not need to use any energy to give life to a physical body, and their spirits have powers far beyond ours. They have the ability to know great many things, and their wills are also different from ours.

When all angels were created, they were given the free will to follow the Creator. When one of the higher angels grasped at the power of God, he was cast out of the presence of God. He did not lead the rebellion alone. Lucifer's hatred of God's authority was joined by a number of angels who joined him and were cast out with him.

The angels who chose God were admitted to the vision of God's glory, called the Beatific Vision. Those who rejected God were refused this vision. Lucifer has a vast knowledge of a great many things, but he cannot see what the outcome will be. This is why he rejoices at the death of Christ, only to be frustrated by the Resurrection. Those who rejected God cannot come to a love of anything since they are so locked into their hatred. They cannot even love themselves.

Angels and demons/fallen angels are limited in their powers. They cannot create matter, but they can manipulate matter and they can move throughout space without limitations. They can work on a human body and manipulate it so that a person sees things that are not there, or is physically controlled by a devil. Usually, if a possession occurs, the person who is possessed has opened him or herself up to the influence of a devil. All devils are powerless before the name of Jesus Christ. All devils will seek to use our pride against us, as Lucifer did with Adam and Eve in the Garden of Eden.

We have a guardian angel who is assigned to our protection. In fact, every year on October 2nd the Church celebrates a Feast Day in honor of Guardian Angels. Three of the verses most commonly associated with guardian angels, in particular, are Matthew 18:10, Psalm 91:4-6, and Exodus 23:20-23. It is important that we pray to our guardian angels, for they protect us from devils who seek to turn our wills against God's.

Now, too often we think of angels – these *heavenly* bodies – in earthly bodily terms, but angels are not human and, therefore, not bound by human constraints. Additionally, humans do not "become" angels when they die. You can become a saint, but not an angel.

Many of us are taught about angels not from the Bible nor from meditations of the saints, but from media: Two wings and a halo, right? Perhaps a white robe? Where does that mental picture come from? Maybe from a painting you've seen, or possibly a movie. Do you know that Scripture doesn't always depict an angel as having two wings? We see six-winged and four-winged angels more than angels with just two (Isaiah 6:2,6, Ezekiel 1:6, Revelation 4:8). We see angels adorned in white and in light, but truthfully, our perception of angels comes more from the Hollywood depictions we've seen than from the word of God. It's vital that we push those stupid movie stereotypes out of our heads, because they negatively affect our truthful perception and reception of angelic intervention.

Angels exist to do the will of God, to be His messengers, guides and protectors — defenders of God's truth. It's important, though, to remember that they are not to be worshipped (Revelation 19:10, 22:9), that's not their role. Again, they exist for the sole purpose of praising and carrying out the will of God.

Your guardian angel is one of God's greatest gifts to you. They are a source of His power. They never leave your side yet they are constantly looking upon the face of God, too. Guardian angels are not only real they are very active. Invite your angel to pray with you, to protect you, to help keep you focused on God and to protect you from evil and from harm.

Prayerfully consider the words of St. Angela Merici who said, "Remember that the devil doesn't sleep, but seeks our ruin in a thousand ways." Just because we go to sleep, doesn't mean the devil rests or stops trying to pull us away from Jesus. As a fallen angel, the devil doesn't need sleep... on the bright side, our guardian angels don't need sleep, either so they can kick fallen angel butt 24/7. (See Revelation 12.)

REFERENCES

Genesis 22:11-12, Acts 8:26, 12:5-15, Matthew 4, 13:39-49, Psalm 34:7, 91:11, Revelation 12:1-18, Mark 1:13, Luke 9:26, 15:10, Genesis 32:1, Hebrews 2:2-2:9, 2 Peter 2:11, Jude 6

CCC 329, 332-336, 350-352, 394-395, 398, 2851-2852

Check out the book "Angels (and Demons)" by Peter Kreeft if you want to have virtually every angel question you've ever wondered about answered in one short paperback.

99. YOUR PURPOSE IN LIFE

One of the most profound moments of my collegiate life came while sharing a basket of buffalo wings with a priest. The conversation we had wasn't particularly theological by any stretch of the imagination, but it had an incredible effect on my life. Between wings, we had talked about everything from Notre Dame football to politics, from new movies to the new U2 album, but it was the last thing he said to me that has never left me. The priest looked me in the eyes and said, "Mark, fish swim, birds fly."

I was perplexed by his statement as he rose from the table and walked away. Over the course of the next couple days, whenever I saw him he repeated that enigmatic statement to me, "Fish swim, birds fly." Finally, three days later I caught up with the priest and he explained it to me. "Fish swim and birds fly... it means that you give glory to God by doing what you are designed to do. And my son, you're not doing it."

The priest called me out in a huge way that day. It's not that I was living an evil or overly sinful life. I wasn't living as holy a life as I could, or surrendering my life to Christ like I was called to. If it had not been for that priest allowing the Holy Spirit to speak through him that day, I never would have gone into ministry. I would have avoided that call from God, possibly for the rest of my life. I was scared to answer God completely because it was just that — my life.

That's where we go wrong most of the time: We look at our lives as our own. We forget who the Creator is in the equation. We ignore the Author of our stories.

God created you for a purpose, for good works (Ephesians 2:10). Likewise, God created you with a purpose that only *you* can fulfill (Jeremiah 1:4-8). You have a calling in life. You have a mission that He designed specifically for you (Psalm 139:14-16).

Often times we fear saying "yes" to God because we don't trust where He is going to take us. We're afraid that His plan is going to be boring, too hard, or too constraining to what we want. He promises us that we have nothing to fear (2 Timothy 1:7), though, and that His plan is not only better than ours (Jeremiah 29:11-12), but will lead to our ultimate joy (John 10:10).

God might be calling you to be a priest or a religious. God might be calling you to marriage. Are you truly open to either? Many people date to find the type of person they want to marry. If you don't also "date" the priesthood or religious life, however, you haven't been truly open to God's call, have you? You might not think that God would want you to be a priest or a religious sister or brother, but He just might. It's time to put it to prayer and "date" every vocation.

God might be calling you to ministry and service. You might have your sights set on a lucrative career, which is fine, but don't make your decisions based upon money. God will take care of you. Put your trust in God (like the back of the money says that we do). If God wants you to serve others, answer His call! In the end you'll not only be faithful, you'll be more joyful. If He is calling you to the secular world, that's great, too! Just be sure that whatever field you end up in, you are a light to all around you. The Church doesn't just need holy priests, religious, and lay ministers, the Church needs holy teachers, lawyers, caregivers, accountants, managers, athletes, artists, musicians, salespeople, trash collectors, and construction workers. Get the idea?

The point is, if you want to be happy and have a fulfilling life, take time now to get to know the Author of that life. He won't steer you wrong, ever.

REFERENCES

Jeremiah 1:4-8, 29:11, Ephesians 2:10, Matthew 6:10, 34, 10:30, 1 Samuel 3:16, Isaiah 6:8, Psalm 143:10, Hebrews 10:7-9

CCC 1701, 1877, 1699, 1533, 1962, 1583, 373, 1603-1604

100. BEING CATHOLIC AND FITTING IN

Earlier in this book we mentioned that there are over 4,000 promises in Scripture. One of the promises that must have left the apostles scratching their heads is given to us by Jesus, and recorded in St. John's Gospel:

"I have said this to you, that in me you may have peace. In the world you have tribulation; but be of good cheer, I have overcome the world." (John 16:33)

Isn't that a little strange? Did you notice how Jesus told us to be "peaceful" as He promises us that we are going to have hard times? That doesn't seem to make a lot of sense on the surface, but it makes perfect sense if you know God.

Your life is not going to be easy, no matter how hard you pray, how often you go to Mass or how fervently you try to love God. He doesn't promise us an easy life and that's okay. Struggles keep us reliant on God. Struggles increase our discipline. Struggles build character. You don't have to worry about a life filled with struggle if God is with you. You need only worry about a life without God.

Many times life is difficult because we are trying to fit into the world, and just don't feel like we do. That's because you were not created for this world, you were created for the next one. Jesus reminds us to be *in* the world but not *of* the world (John 15:18-19).

To be holy means to be "set apart." As you allow God to make you more and more holy, you are allowing God to set your life apart even more. That doesn't mean you have to go live a secluded life by yourself though, it means that your life stands out, as a light to all those in the world trapped in darkness. The goal is not to fit in, it's to stand out (humbly) in holiness and in love.

This call to holiness shouldn't stress you, it should excite you. A good portion of our lives are spent stressing about things that already happened (which we can't change) or about things that might happen (which we can't control). God doesn't want you to be filled with anxiety and stress (Matthew 6:34). Share your days with Him. Share your stresses with Him. Spend time talking (and more importantly) listening to Him. Seek out true friendships (Sirach 6:14) and community with others who believe in God like you do, and who are seeking God as you are (2 Corinthians 6:14).

Life Teen wants to help support you and to foster that community of support. Go on our website and find a parish in your area. Check out the national events that we host, spend some time at our summer camps and look for regional prayer meetings and training opportunities coming to your area. Become a member of our online community. Life Teen is here to walk with you as we all journey toward Christ!

End Notes

[1] Mark Hart, *Blessed are the Bored in Spirit*
(Cincinnati, OH: Servant Books)

[2] Mark Hart, T3: *The Teen Timeline*
(West Chester, PA: Ascension Press)

[3] Mark Hart, *Ask the Bible Geek*
(Cincinnati, OH: Servant Books)

[4] Constitution on Sacred Liturgy VII, 112

[5] Mark Hart, *Blessed are the Bored in Spirit*
(Cincinnati, OH: Servant Books)

[6] Ibid.

[7] Brian Butler, Jason Evert, and Crystalina Evert,
Theology of the Body for Teens
(West Chester, PA: Ascension Press)

[8] Mark Hart, *Blessed are the Bored in Spirit*
(Cincinnati, OH: Servant Books)

[9] The original source of these statistics are from the
Center for Media and Public affairs, Washington, D.C.

APPENDIX

PRAYERS YOU SHOULD KNOW

Here is a list of Catholic prayers we say frequently and would bless your prayer life to know. If you don't know them, don't be ashamed to learn them. If you do know them, don't just recite them but be sure to pray them. Remember, prayer is more than a recitation of words, prayer is a conversation with our God.

APOSTLE'S CREED

I believe in God, the Father Almighty, Creator of heaven and earth and in Jesus Christ, His only Son, our Lord; Who was conceived by the Holy Spirit, born of the Virgin Mary, suffered under Pontius Pilate, was crucified, died, and was buried, He descended into hell; the third day He arose again from the dead; He ascended into Heaven, and sits at the right hand of God, the Father Almighty, from there He shall come to judge the living and the dead. I believe in the Holy Spirit, the Holy Catholic Church, the communion of saints, the forgiveness of sins, the resurrection of the body, and life everlasting. Amen.

THE LORD'S PRAYER

Our Father, Who art in Heaven, hallowed be Thy name; Thy Kingdom come, Thy will be done on earth as it is in Heaven. Give us this day our daily bread; and forgive us our trespasses as we forgive those who trespass against us; and lead us not into temptation, but deliver us from evil. Amen.

HAIL MARY

Hail Mary, full of grace, the Lord is with thee, blessed art thou amongst women and blessed is the fruit of thy womb, Jesus. Holy Mary Mother of God, pray for us sinners now and at the hour of our death. Amen.

THE DOXOLOGY (GLORY BE)

All Glory be to the Father, the Son and the Holy Spirit, as it was in the beginning, is now and ever shall be, a world without end. Amen.

SALVE REGINA (HAIL HOLY QUEEN)

Hail Holy Queen, Mother of Mercy, our life our sweetness and our hope. To thee do we cry, poor banished children of Eve; To thee do we send up our sighs, mourning and weeping in this valley of tears. Turn then, most gracious advocate, thine eyes of mercy toward us and after this our exile show unto us the blessed fruit of thy womb, Jesus. O clement, O loving, O sweet Virgin Mary! Pray for us, O holy Mother of God. That we may be made worthy of the promises of Christ.

MEMORARE

Remember, O most gracious Virgin Mary that never was it known that anyone who fled to your protection, implored your help, or sought your intercession was left unaided. Inspired with this confidence, we fly to you, O Virgin of virgins, our mother. To you we come; before you we stand, sinful and sorrowful. O Mother of the Word Incarnate, despise not our petitions, but in Your mercy, hear and answer us. Amen.

ST. MICHAEL PRAYER

St. Michael, the Archangel, defend us in battle. Be our safeguard against the wickedness and snares of the devil. May God rebuke him, we humbly pray; and do you, O Prince of the heavenly host, by the power of God cast into hell Satan and all the evil spirits who wander through the world seeking the ruin of souls. Amen.

NICENE CREED

I believe in one God,
the Father almighty,
maker of heaven and earth,
of all things visible and invisible.

I believe in one Lord Jesus Christ,
the Only Begotten Son of God,
born of the Father before all ages.
God from God, Light from Light,
true God from true God,
begotten, not made, consubstantial with the Father;
through him all things were made.
For us men and for our salvation
he came down from heaven,
and by the Holy Spirit was incarnate of the Virgin Mary,
and became man.
For our sake he was crucified under Pontius Pilate,
he suffered death and was buried,
and rose again on the third day
in accordance with the Scriptures.
He ascended into heaven
and is seated at the right hand of the
Father.

He will come again in glory
to judge the living and the dead
and his kingdom will have no end.

I believe in the Holy Spirit, the Lord, the giver of life,
who proceeds from the Father and the Son,
who with the Father and the Son is adored and glorified,
who has spoken through the prophets.

I believe in one, holy, catholic and apostolic Church.
I confess one Baptism for the forgiveness of sins
and I look forward to the resurrection of the dead
and the life of the world to come. Amen.

THE HOLY ROSARY

The rosary is divided into four sets of Mysteries: Joyful, Luminous, Sorrowful, and Glorious. It is intended, as we pray each "Mystery," that we meditate on the meaning of the event in the life of Christ and Mary, and also on the event in our own lives. Each Mystery has five decades and each decade is prayed upon in the following order: Our Father, Hail Mary, and the Glory Be. There are other prayers added onto the beginning and end of the rosary such as the Apostle's Creed and the Hail Holy Queen.

The mysteries:

JOYFUL

1. The Annunciation
2. The Visitation
3. The Nativity of Jesus
4. The Presentation of Jesus
5. The Finding of Jesus

LUMINOUS

1. The Baptism of Jesus
2. The Miracle at Cana
3. The Proclamation of the Kingdom
4. The Transfiguration
5. The Institution of the Eucharist

SORROWFUL

1. The Agony in the Garden
2. The Scourging at the Pillar
3. The Crowning with Thorns
4. The Carrying of the Cross
5. The Crucifixion

GLORIOUS

1. The Resurrection
2. The Ascension of Jesus
3. The Descent of the Holy Spirit
4. The Assumption of Mary
5. The Coronation of Mary

The prayer order:

Sign of the Cross

Apostles Creed

Our Father – First Bead
Three Hail Marys – Three beads
- One for an increase in Faith
- One for an increase in Hope
- One for an increase in Love

Glory Be – Fifth bead

First Mystery:
Our Father – single bead
10 Hail Mary - 10 beads
Glory Be

Second Mystery:
Our Father – single bead
10 Hail Mary – 10 beads
Glory Be

Third Mystery:
Our Father – single bead
10 Hail Mary – 10 beads
Glory Be

Fourth Mystery:
Our Father – single bead
10 Hail Mary – 10 beads
Glory Be

Fifth Mystery:
Our Father – single bead
10 Hail Mary – 10 beads
Glory Be
Hail Holy Queen

EXPLAINING THE CATHOLIC FAITH WITH THE SCRIPTURES

The Catholic Church put the Bible together. The Church didn't come out of the (written) Gospels; the Gospels came out of the Church. The New Testament wasn't written immediately following the Resurrection, it took over two decades before St. Paul and the Gospel writers began writing. In addition, the New Testament (as we know it) wasn't compiled until a few hundred years later (in its canonical form).

Our Church believes that the Bible is one source (not the only source) of Divine Revelation. The Sacred Scriptures work "in conjunction" with the living, oral Tradition of the Church, lived by Christ and His apostles and entrusted to the Church through the power and protection of the Holy Spirit. The two were never meant to be separated.

The sad truth is that many Catholics shy away from defending the faith because they don't know how to answer or where to look to get the answers. The answers, however, are probably closer than you think. Be sure to check your Bible for footnotes, they are an incredible aid in your comprehension of a passage. In addition, the *Catechism of the Catholic Church* is a book you should always have on hand and in hand. Get to know your way around the *Catechism* and use it frequently. You will be amazed at the wealth of information contained within it.

For starters, though, here is a "quick reference" guide to which Scriptures you can use to explain some of what we believe as Roman Catholics. It is intended to be used along with your *Catechism*, to help communicate the depths and richness of the Church's teachings on these subjects. This is in no way the complete list, but rather a list of 10 commonly questioned Catholic doctrines/ disciplines and Scripture verses related to each:

1. The Blessed Virgin Mary
Luke 1:28
Luke 1:30,34
Luke 1:42
John 19:26
Genesis 3:15

2. The Papacy
Matthew 16:180
Luke 22:32
John 20:23, 21:17
Acts 1:13-26
Acts 8:21
Acts 15:7, 28
1 Timothy 3:1, 8
1 Timothy 5:17

3. The Bible and Tradition
Mark 13:31
Mark 16:15
John 21:25
Romans 10:17
1 Corinthians 11:2
2 Thessalonians 2:15, 3:6

2 Timothy 1:13, 2:2
2 Peter 1:20

4. Faith and Works
Matthew 19:16-17
John 14:15
Romans 2:5-8
1 Corinthians 13:2
Galatians 5:6
Ephesians 2:8-10
Colossians 3:24-25
James 2:24-26
Revelation 20:12-13

5. Eucharist
Matthew 26:26
John 1:29
John 6:35-71
1 Corinthians 2:14-3:4
1 Corinthians 5:7, 10:16
1 Corinthians 11:23-29
Exodus 12:8, 46

6. Purgatory
Matthew 5:26, 48
Matthew 12:32-36
1 Corinthians 3:15
1 Corinthians 15:29-30
2 Timothy 1:16-18
James 3:2
1 Peter 3:18-20, 4:6
1 John 5:16-17
Revelation 21-27

2 Maccabees 12:44-46

7. Mary and the Saints
Luke 16:19-30
Romans 8:35-39, 15:30
1 Corinthians 12:12-27
Ephesians 6:18-19
1 Thessalonians 1:5-8
1 Timothy 2:1-7
Hebrews 12:1, 13:7
1 John 3:2
Galatians 6:10

8. Reconciliation
Matthew 9:2-8
Matthew 18:18
John 20:22-23
2 Corinthians 5:17-20
James 5:13-16
1 John 5:16

9. Salvation
Matthew 7:21, 10:22
Romans 8:24, 11:22
1 Corinthians 9:27, 10:11-12
Galatians 5:4
Ephesians 2:5, 8
Philippians 2:12
2 Timothy 1:9, 2:11-13
Hebrews 10:26-27
1 Peter 1:9

10. The Priesthood

Matthew 19:19
Luke 14:26
Acts 7:2
Acts 21:40, 22:1
Romans 4:16-17
1 Corinthians 4:14-15
1 Thessalonians 2:11
Hebrews 12:7-9
1 John 2:13-14

Remember, the Roman Catholic Church has a long tradition — the longest in fact. We are the only Church that was founded by Christ Himself (Matthew 16:16-20). Take some time to thank God for the gift of His Church and for the grace that you were born into through your conception, His cross, your Baptism, and the Sacraments. Make the time to study the footnotes in your Bible, the *Catechism of the Catholic Church*, and other Church documents — they are gifts to us, to help us accurately "unpack" the mysteries and truths of God contained in the Sacred Scriptures and in our Church.

SUGGESTED READING

THE BLESSED VIRGIN MARY
The World's First Love – Venerable Archbishop Fulton Sheen
That One Girl – Christina Mead
The New Rosary in Scripture – Edward Sri
Full of Grace – Life Teen

THE EXISTENCE OF GOD
Because God is Real - Peter Kreeft
Summa Theologica - St. Thomas Aquinas
A Map of Life - Frank Sheed
The Language of God: A Scientist Presents Evidence for Belief - Francis S. Collins
Mere Christianity - C.S. Lewis
Theology for Beginners - Frank Sheed
The Case for Christ - Lee Strobel

SALVATION
Heaven, the Heart's Deepest Longing - Peter Kreeft
Mere Christianity - C.S. Lewis
Born Fundamentalist, Born Again Catholic - David Currie
Jesus of Nazareth: Holy Week – Pope Emeritus Benedict XVI

MAGISTERIUM
The Fathers of the Church: An Introduction to the First Christian Teachers - Mike Aquilina
Rise Let Us Be On Our Way – Pope Saint John Paul II
Pope Fiction: Answers to 30 Myths and Misconceptions About the Papacy - Patrick Madrid

Jesus, Peter & the Keys: A Scriptural Handbook on the Papacy - Scott Butler

Women and the Priesthood - Peter Kreeft and Alice von Hildebrand

THE CHURCH

A Compact History of the Catholic Church - Alan Schreck

Triumph: The Power and the Glory of the Catholic Church - H.W. Crocker

Fundamentals of the Faith - Peter Kreeft

A Man for All Seasons - Robert Bolt

Nothing But the Truth - Karl Keating

Truth and Tolerance: Christian Belief and World Religions – Pope Emeritus Benedict XVI

Catholic for a Reason I, II - ed. Scott Hahn

SCRIPTURES

A Father Who Keeps His Promises - Scott Hahn

You Can Read and Understand the Bible - Peter Kreeft

Bible Basics for Catholics – John Bergsma

To Know Christ Jesus - Frank Sheed

The Lamb's Supper - Scott Hahn

Making Senses Out of Scripture: Reading the Bible As the First Christians Did - Mark Shea

Where we Got the Bible - Henry G. Graham

Ask the Bible Geek - Mark Hart

Ask the Bible Geek 2 - Mark Hart

SACRAMENTS

Jesus of Nazareth - Pope Emeritus Benedict XVI

Lord, Have Mercy - Scott Hahn

Love and Responsibility – Pope Saint John Paul II

Essential Catholic Handbook of the Sacraments –
Redemptorist Pastoral Publication

THE MASS
Images of Hope - Pope Emeritus Benedict XVI
The Lamb's Supper - Scott Hahn
Behold the Mystery – Mark Hart
Spirit of Liturgy – Pope Emeritus Benedict XVI

PRAYER
The Little Way of St. Theresa of Liseux: Readings for Prayer and Meditation
Introduction to the Devout Life - St. Francis de Sales
Prayer for Beginners - Peter Kreeft
The "R" Father – Mark Hart
Peace of Soul – Venerable Archbishop Fulton Sheen
Letters to a Young Catholic – George Weigel

MORALITY
Back to Virtue - Peter Kreeft
Man's Search for Meaning - Victor Frankl
Refutation of Moral Relativism - Peter Kreeft
Humanae Vitae - Pope Paul VI
Theology and Sanity - Frank Sheed
Theology of the Body for Beginners - Christopher West
Compendium of the Catechism of the Catholic Church
Summa Theologica - St. Thomas Aquinas
A Theology of the Body – Pope Saint John Paul II
The Good News about Sex and Marriage - Christopher West